Upstairs at the Strand

Upstairs at the *STRAND*

* * *

Writers in Conversation at the Legendary Bookstore

EDITED BY
Jessica Strand &
Andrea Aguilar

W. W. NORTON & COMPANY
Independent Publishers Since 1923
NEW YORK LONDON

Printed in the United States of America
First Edition

For information about special discounts for bulk purchases, please contact W. W. Norton Special Sales at specialsales@wwnorton.com or 800-233-4830

Manufacturing by Quad Graphics, Fairfield
Book design by Brian Mulligan
Production manager: Louise Mattarelliano

ISBN 978-0-393-35208-5 (pbk.)

W. W. Norton & Company, Inc.
500 Fifth Avenue, New York, N.Y. 10110
www.wwnorton.com

W. W. Norton & Company Ltd.
Castle House, 75/76 Wells Street, London W1T 3QT

1 2 3 4 5 6 7 8 9 0

To Dad, always

Contents

Introduction

For nearly ninety years, the Strand has been a New York institution, a mecca for readers across the five boroughs and beyond. It began in 1927, when Benjamin Bass, a devoted reader and lover of the arts, opened a small secondhand bookstore on Book Row, the stretch of Fourth Avenue between Fourteenth Street and Astor Place then known for its density of bookshops. Bass put up $300 of his own money, borrowed another $300 from a friend, and opened the Strand Book Store, named for the street in London. With Bass's shrewd business sense and deep knowledge of books, the Strand soon attracted a following, and even as most stores on Book Row had closed, the store thrived. In 1956, Bass moved the store to bigger digs around the corner, at the corner of Broadway and Twelfth Street, where it stands today as Book Row's sole survivor.

Over the years, floors were added, sections and shelves were expanded, order was brought from the chaos. (Perhaps the only physical detail that remains untouched is a ground-floor column that stands as a memento to the past.) The store is still run by the Bass family: Bass's son Fred joined the fold, and in turn so, too, did Fred's daughter Nancy. Even as the store has grown—weathering the rise of big chain bookstores and then the Internet—the Strand's identity has remained well defined. "The Strand," as Fran Lebowitz has said, "is a monument to the immortality of the written word and hence beloved writers." It is an enormous, overstuffed place where just about any book can be found, even—and especially—the one you didn't know you were looking for. Not for nothing do the store's red awnings boast 18 MILES OF BOOKS. And it is just as much a place to find people as it is books: from its eccentric staff, deeply in love with books, to the writers, intellectuals, and artists who have long gathered there, to the New Yorkers and tourists of every stripe roaming the stacks. As Pete Hamill has written, the Strand is "an institution . . . as mixed, as diverse, as democratic, as intellectual, as high and low as the city itself . . . The Strand is [New York's] great meeting corner."

The last floor to be added to the store was the Rare Book Room, in 2003. The walls of the loft-like space are covered in floor-to-ceiling shelves filled with hard-to-find and unusual volumes—from signed first editions of beloved twentieth century novels to small-run art books to mysterious, ancient tomes on the occult. Oriental rugs in deep maroons and blues dot the floor along with overstuffed leather chairs—like the library of some eccentric, prodigious collector.

It was this feeling—the serendipity, the variety, the happy collision of books, ideas, and people—that we tried to capture in our reading series up in the Rare Book Room. The goal was to match writers with other writers: two (or more) equals on stage for freewheeling, candid conversations on their work, their craft, their likes, their dislikes. Some of the conversations gathered here are between old, dear friends, like Mark Strand and Charles Wright, or Hilton Als and Junot Díaz, or

Tina Chang and Tracy K. Smith. Others feature great admirers who had never met (or met only briefly), like Renata Adler and David Shields, or Téa Obreht and Charles Simic. In all cases, the result is every bit as electrifying and edifying as the store itself.

—Jessica Strand

Upstairs at the Strand

1

Deborah Eisenberg & George Saunders

WITH LUCAS WITTMANN

LUCAS WITTMANN

I've been struck by how both of you are such incredibly articulate, expressive people, and yet you are able to capture brilliantly how we are all so inexpressive, how inarticulate and often unable to communicate we can be. Deborah, I was looking at one of your short stories and noted down some phrases that you use, like "vaguely severe" and "kind of churchy." This of course is how we all think and talk, when we are not having a chance to compose ourselves. I was curious to know how you were able to capture those brief moments of inexpressiveness.

DEBORAH EISENBERG

Actually, inarticulateness comes very naturally to me.

LUCAS WITTMANN

You're proving that not to be true.

DEBORAH EISENBERG

The story in which those particular phrases occur is very "voice-y," and it was fun to utilize the complete confusion of natural speech. I enjoy doing it a lot. I don't know what else to say about it, it's just fun.

GEORGE SAUNDERS

It is fun. I grew up in Chicago, and one of my early experiences was watching the male neighbors, who were a little drunk but very earnest. They would have, obviously, fully developed emotional lives and longings, but then there would be kind of a crimped output valve. If someone tried to say that they loved you or that they found you outstanding, they would say, "You jag-off! You! You!" and they'd pretend to knee you in the groin. You come to understand that diction. One of my true breakthrough moments in writing was when I realized that this was actually a form of poetry, that any diction that you overflow, even if it's inefficient on the surface, becomes beautiful when you kind of put the screws to it a little bit.

LUCAS WITTMANN

George, when you read out loud you use those voices, but do you write in those kind of voices, too?

GEORGE SAUNDERS

I write in a lot better ones. I've got three voices that I do: a working-class guy, a rich guy, and a duck—I can do a pretty good duck. When I'm writing I hear them very well and when they come out, you sort of compromise the solution.

LUCAS WITTMANN

I'd like to ask you both about how you started writing. Deborah, with you, it was when you quit smoking, is that right?

DEBORAH EISENBERG

When I quit smoking, absolutely. It had to be one or the other, I guess. I was a very, very heavy smoker, and I absolutely loved smoking. But it became evident for various reasons that I had to quit. When I did I completely fell totally apart, because I was entirely structured around nicotine. I mean, nicotine was my blood, my life. A new person started to formulate. I was a monstrous person. I was a monster. It was just so awful. It's horrible, it's awful. But yes, if you smoke, do quit.

LUCAS WITTMANN

George, in your case you found your voice while you were on a conference call, yes?

GEORGE SAUNDERS

I had been working for a long time. I had a medical condition called a "Hemingway boner." I just loved him. I loved him! I did that thing that a lot of young writers do, where you take your interesting experiences and try to cram them down your reader's throat, in some other writer's voice. Of course, it didn't work.

Then one day I was at this tech-writing job, and I was so bored that I jotted down these Seuss poems, kind of a little perverse, kind of like da-da-da-da-da-DA, da-da-da-da-da-DA. There's this great reader I have—my wife—I mean she's really brilliant, and just before this happened I'd written a book called *La Boda de Eduardo*, which I think means *Ed's Wedding*. It must have been a seven-hundred-page book. When I gave it to her, like all writers, I said, "I'll just let you take your time with this. I'll check in tomorrow." Two minutes later, I was under the table and looking up. She was on page three and had her head in her hands. So then I was writing these Dr. Seuss poems, and from the other room I heard her laughing. I understood it was okay to be a little funny, be a little high-velocity, to let what I considered all these low, working-class attributes, like humor and stuff, in. It was just like going around a corner after that.

LUCAS WITTMANN

Speaking of the word "class" . . . George, you have an interest in what's happening to the middle class. Maybe it's a nostalgia, a distant thing that never really was? What draws you to explore that? And Deborah, did you grow up in that?

DEBORAH EISENBERG

I certainly did. When I was growing up, there was a huge middle class, that's what this country was. And it was very stable. One assumed that there would always be a middle class. It had many, many fascinations, and many frustrating and disturbing elements. Now, to see it become incredibly eroded, and to feel that we're on this huge planetary cliff of every sort, class, climate, everything . . . it couldn't be more terrifying, more fascinating. Well, it's just riveting.

LUCAS WITTMANN

We talk about it but in a kind of half-way.

DEBORAH EISENBERG

Things are moving very, very fast. Who can understand what's going on?

GEORGE SAUNDERS

In my class in Syracuse I teach Deborah's *Twilight of the Superheroes.* What the kids love about it is that there's this incredibly funny, intelligent surface and then there are those deep underlying ideas that come up. I always find that with your work, that I step into it and I can't stop. You are writing about those things, but charm always comes first. My students fall in love with your work. I feel that sometimes when we discuss writing, it tends to be a little conceptual and reductive. What I'm trying to tell my students is that you can get themes and concepts and moralities, but you first have to charm the reader. You're such a master of that.

DEBORAH EISENBERG

Back at you.

LUCAS WITTMANN

And the middle class? You can't quite dodge it entirely.

GEORGE SAUNDERS

In that Hemingway period I mentioned, I found out that the same minute I had an idea about what I wanted to write, life would go out of it. I'm a Bear of Little Brain, as Winnie the Pooh would say. My challenge is to try to keep the themes out of what I'm writing as long as possible. I often use this quote that I love by Gerald Stern. He said something like, "If you start out to write a poem about two dogs fucking, and you write a poem about two dogs fucking, then you've written a poem about two dogs fucking." Einstein said it better: "No worthy problem is ever solved on the plane of its original conception." To me that means that if I get an idea about a story, and I think, "Oh, I'm writing about the lower middle class," then I better be careful. You see, if that's all you do, that's all you've done. Rather, it's got more integrity if it comes in of its own accord. When you start out to do this, it somehow seems it falls flat.

LUCAS WITTMANN

You mentioned teaching Deborah's work. You both teach? Neither of you were taught. I'm curious how you compare being self-taught and teaching writing.

GEORGE SAUNDERS

I did go through an MFA program, at Syracuse. With Tobias Wolff and Douglas Unger. I had it handed to me, on a silver platter. They just told me what to do and I did it. It's easy, once you know the secret.

DEBORAH EISENBERG

I find it very puzzling to be teaching writing without ever having learned to write. I mostly define the task of teaching writing as trying to persuade students that there actually are no rules. That it can't be learned in exactly that way. It's an interesting analogy to what George was saying about imposing ideas on a piece of fiction or starting with an idea. You have to go about it in a much more internal way. The school model is a little dangerous, for writing students. What I have to offer is to say, "This is a false model."

GEORGE SAUNDERS

I just got an email from Syracuse that says that there are six hundred applications for six spots this year. At that level you don't have to teach them anything in particular, you have to get them up to their highest personal level. I find it's psychological work. You get to know the person over the three years and at some critical point you can say something or make an edit and that points out at a deep level that they're right about something or that they're barking up the wrong tree. It's very pleasant work, but I don't think there's methodology for sure.

LUCAS WITTMANN

How have you evolved as writers?

GEORGE SAUNDERS

When I was younger, I was for some stupid reason really taken aback by the realization that capitalism could be harsh. It had never occurred to me before. So my work tended to be a little preoccupied with that notion, maybe. My wife and I fell head over heels, and had our daughters pretty quickly. Now we've been married for twenty-six years and our daughters are grown up and wonderful. So lately my feeling is there ought to be a place for some fictional corollary of the fact that sometimes things actually work. Sometimes in fiction you put the baby near the cliff. And in this latest book of mine [*Tenth of December*], the baby doesn't quite go over. Earlier it would have, earlier it would have gone over the cliff. Or into the latrine. An artist can sometimes represent the idea that things can be wonderful.

DEBORAH EISENBERG

I don't think my writing has gotten more cheerful, at all. It's possibly gotten a little more complicated. That's the only difference. I keep trying, trying, trying to express inexpressible things. I try to be able to articulate a few more of the contingencies, and strange nuances of life, as I go along.

LUCAS WITTMANN

You are both short story writers. And they say the short story is dead but this room is packed. You're proof that it's not. Why do you write short stories? Have you tried novels? Are you against them?

GEORGE SAUNDERS

This year I came across that Flannery O'Connor line, "The writer can choose what he writes about but he cannot choose what he is able to make live." When a story is eight pages, I get it. I feel that I can make that live. I like the idea of expanding or developing, but when I get there, there's no strong idea. I've got a vigorous inner nun that says, "Why are you taking so long, Mr. Saunders? What do you know?" My stuff, when it works, is like a windup toy. You wind it up and it hides under the couch as quickly as possible. It can even take only one wrong turn and the energy goes down and it's dull. I'm not thrilled with this—with this idea of working from a limited skill-set—but I'm resigned to it.

DEBORAH EISENBERG

Things take me forever to write, too. I love compression. Also, I feel a kind of almost squeamishness of taking even five words longer than I need. It offends my sensibility, in a way. It's not that I don't like to read long things. I do, I love to read long things. But when I'm working that's how I feel.

LUCAS WITTMANN

George, at the beginning of the story "Victory Lap," there's this line: "Can goodness win?" It's kind of an overarching question in your work.

GEORGE SAUNDERS

Why not? Yes, it can win. But it can also lose—can get humiliated. It can also cause other people problems, by morphing into self-righteousness. I think what a fiction writer does is represent different viewpoints vividly. And without necessarily seeming to prefer one over the other. "Can goodness win?"

"Yes, it does all the time." "No, it cannot: it loses all the time." Both true. There's this passage in Gorky's memoirs, where he takes a walk with Tolstoy in Russia—where they, being Russian, often walked—and there are these Hussars coming toward them. Tolstoy at this point is like a hundred and eighty and newly celibate, but he points out that those Hussars represent all that's wrong with Russia: the arrogance, the aggression, the blind self-confidence. "Trust me," is the sense of what he's saying, "those traits will be the ruin of Russia." Gorky thinks this is brilliant. And then the Hussars pass by with their swords clanking and their cologne. And Tolstoy turns on his heels, watches them go, and says, "On the other hand, that's everything that's *good* about us: the pride, the self-assertion, the confidence in a better future." Gorky says, "Well, Leo, which is it?" And Tolstoy just sort of smiles, walks off. No answer. So . . . they're both true, at once. Leave it just like that. See how long you can stay in that space, where both things are true. You, little mind, actually don't have to *decide*. That's a great place to try to be. And for a fiction writer, that's the best place to be: you've put two apparently opposing truths in the air and you're just letting them hang there, knowing that the real truth is . . . that opposition.

LUCAS WITTMANN

You both come across as very sane, happy people. Your stories are populated by characters who are complicated, or are tragic, and torn. Do you get your emotions out on the page?

DEBORAH EISENBERG

People, you know, have interiors. One doesn't just walk around saying, *Rrrrr!* We have all kinds of things going on. People have experiences, and people have feelings. I would say that in one's life, one does a certain amount of choosing about how one is going to be.

LUCAS WITTMANN

I wanted to ask Deborah about the Passivity Man, and how 9/11 is treated in one of your stories obliquely, but at times directly, too.

DEBORAH EISENBERG

I don't normally take notes, or keep a journal. But I started taking notes on that night, September 11th, 2001, because I felt that things were going to start changing immediately, as they did. I felt that it would be impossible to remember, accurately, what one's experience was. The story took me three years to write. All that material had to be translated into something that was useful for fiction. I didn't start writing a piece of fiction about it at all, but I was writing fiction. I couldn't get rid of the horrible sensation of falsifying history practically as it's rolling by underfoot. I just did not want to falsify it. The superhero Lucas mentioned is a comic book character that's being invented by one of my characters. I don't know how that developed or got in.

Questions from the Audience

Do you believe that moniker is destiny? Deborah, refresh my memory—what did Deborah do in the Bible? George, which George would you be the reincarnation of?

GEORGE SAUNDERS

Clooney.

DEBORAH EISENBERG

Deborah was a judge, as I remember, but I don't really remember.

George, you wrote some essays about authors like Kurt Vonnegut and Mark Twain. Why? And Deborah, do you have any interest in pursuing any other nonfiction or essay writing? You wrote some rather nice book reviews of some great Central European novels.

GEORGE SAUNDERS

After my second book, I felt that I'd gotten a little cornered. Not that I couldn't write, but I was a little stuck, aesthetically. I felt that if I wrote some other stuff it might break the jam. I feel intuitively that if you're cramped you just have to lurch. Sometimes going into another form will loosen up the game a bit. At one point I got the fiction mojo back. It's kind of a survival tactic—you just have to keep moving around.

DEBORAH EISENBERG

My experience was somewhat similar. I ran aground, I could not write any fiction that interested me, and I was given the opportunity to write some of those essays. Not a bunch, I mean one—I was given one, and then another, and another. I found it very refreshing and also very taxing. It took much longer than I expected. This kind of writing is interesting and very satisfying, because you have a much clearer idea of what the task is than you do with fiction. With fiction the problem, ultimately, is to invent the task.

When you guys hit a block in a piece, what tactics do you use to overcome that? Do you maybe change the point of view, put some distance, or just work on another piece?

GEORGE SAUNDERS

The only frank advice I can offer would be that, maybe, you can say to yourself that the obstacle is part of it. It's not that you're the one person who doesn't understand story craft. That block is often the story going, "I'm not enough yet. Can you please help me expand?" It takes a certain amount of patience, maybe a little sense of humor, to acknowledge that this is happening, and that it is all right. It's part of the process, rather than trauma—no use in simply blaming yourself for "doing it wrong."

DEBORAH EISENBERG

There are obstacles, there just are. But they are information, in a way. There's nothing you can do except be very patient. And yes, switching point of view is a good idea, switching settings. Just play, try to have a little fun. Obstacles are part of the process, and the obstacle that you hit is information.

What stories do you always teach?

DEBORAH EISENBERG

I tend not to teach contemporary stories, but all kinds of other things. Let's start with "Earthquake in Chile," by Von Kleist, a great story. Isaac Babel stories are wonderful. I've taught some Joyce, some Faulkner, the usual suspects. Also Bolaño. And various things that my students might not encounter on their own.

GEORGE SAUNDERS

I have this one exercise. It's Hemingway, speaking of him. You take that story "Indian Camp." It's maybe eight pages or something. You divide it into two-page bits. I give them the first two pages. And we read in class and talk about it for way too long, longer than they're content with. And you say, What's up here? What has Hemingway got going in these first two pages? And then you give them the second two pages, and you see the way that story is just pure escalation. There's nothing in that story that just sits, stable. And by the end they're ready to kill you (because they want so badly to get to the end), but you can say, just before you hand out that last chunk: Okay, this is a masterpiece, you've got a page and a half left, is there anything left to do? And they say, No, not really, and then he does it anyway.

George, do you feel that there are any stories or characters that you've created that are really close to your heart?

GEORGE SAUNDERS

I don't have characters or stories that really are. To me the proper thing is to be into it at the time, even crazily, to the point where even a comma is a fighting thing, to the point where you feel that the people in it are real. But the trick is to quickly get rid of it afterwards. You kind of go, "Ah, I failed again, time to go."

How many stories are you working on at a time?

DEBORAH EISENBERG

I think I'm working on one. I hope I'm working on one.

GEORGE SAUNDERS

When I'm going, I usually have two or three things on my desk, and see which one is most interesting. Then at some point, one of them surges ahead, and I kind of just lock down on that.

How much of your process is overwriting? Is it intentional?

GEORGE SAUNDERS

To what extent do we overwrite to get the final thing?

DEBORAH EISENBERG

I have to write reams and reams. Most of what I do is cutting.

GEORGE SAUNDERS

For voice-driven stories, I have to go, like, one hundred units to get twenty-five.

George, I think in Tenth of December *there's a theme about characters and the special destinies they imagine for themselves, that might not come to pass, or that may never give expression to themselves as fully as possible, or as they imagined. But your special destiny has come to pass. Can you speak about this irony?*

GEORGE SAUNDERS

For me it's not so much about special destiny but the moment-by-moment failure of one's habitual approach. You could be a king or you could be a peasant, but you've got this thing going on in your mind that's delusional. No matter what you're doing, this victory narrative is not important; what's important is that at any given moment you're failing to see the way things actually are. The manifestation is that you're failing to be kind. You're anxious. You're neurotic. I don't think it's so much about external things. I think you could be a very happy, high-functioning person and still note the moment-to-moment failures. I think you're right about what the book is about, but I wouldn't tie it to external wins and losses.

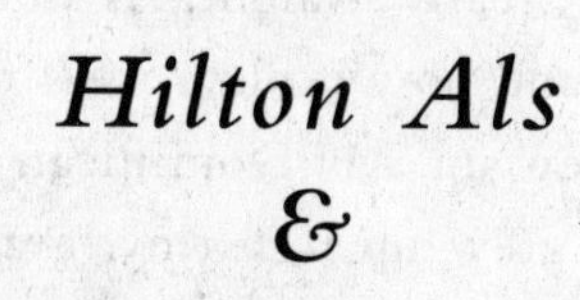

Hilton Als & Junot Díaz

HILTON ALS

Junot—reviewers, who are generally hemmed in by political correctness, tend to avoid the *pato*. I'm a *pato*, and I don't feel demeaned or criticized by this epithet in your works, since I come from the same world. Can you talk to us a bit about the machismo?

JUNOT DÍAZ

This is a foundational question, really interesting. When I think about the political unconsciousness of masculinity, it's queerness. So the first book I ever wrote was an essay, a first pass at a specific kind of masculinity, and I thought I'd name the book after the queerest story in the collection. But from everything I've seen, I don't think a single critic mentioned it. It was weird, such an obvious lacuna.

Anyway, it's something that I'm deeply interested in, and the project continued in *Oscar Wao*. You don't need to be a scholar to see this character as a very queer subject. But I can't imagine masculinity without this sort of tissue that is used to prevent any thought about its own queerness. Masculinity comes with a beard attached, so it can pretend that everything is really, really straight. As an artist, I was really interested in that, and how it plays itself out in the kind of culture where I grew up. My Dominican background is no one else's, guys. I grew up in a tiny, granularly particular place and time, with a particular set of people. There is no universal claim, and I hope you get that. This was such a present discussion when I was growing up, that later I had to jump into it.

HILTON ALS

When we were having Chinese food around Christmastime, you showed me pictures of a trip to the Dominican Republic. There was a table of queens, and I pointed out that they looked really nice and asked if they were your friends. You said they were kind of your only friends down there, because they could do sensitivity, and at the same time they could also play into the culture. That was a great discussion we had about masculinity as a kind of drag.

JUNOT DÍAZ

Without *any* question. In Santo Domingo, there are these kind of performative, hyper-masculine spaces where you can't have an openly gay friend. That's the rule. Of course, the point is, you're supposed to break all that shit. If people see you're hanging out with a queen, they're going to be like, "You're gay." It's a way to actively patrol this. Where I grew up in New Jersey, the homo-social was okay, as long as we called it straight. It was okay that you got naked and wrestled with your boys, but that was called a sport.

On the other hand, my life in Santo Domingo makes it really, really explicit. The friends that I have down there, who have borne the full wrath of a culture, tend to be more interested in discussing things in explicit terms. And if you're an artist, the least helpful friends are people who say things like, "I don't think there's racism." It's okay if they are your family members, because you cannot disown your family in the ways you should be able to. My entire family, they're like, "Racism? I just don't like niggers."

HILTON ALS

My brother is very light-skinned, and my West Indian grandmother would tell me to get out of the sun, because I had had enough of it. Haitian and Dominican cultures, in terms of the color scale, can be deeply wounding. It took me many years of growing up and thinking that this was some sort of internalized craziness. Throughout your books, they're always talking about the color scale. One of the things that I find very brave is that you say it, and then let the characters illustrate it.

JUNOT DÍAZ

I'm not jumping to some conclusion about some abstract culture. You and I come from backgrounds where people were echo chambers for a lot of the cultural, racial sort of defaults. People would say wild things explicitly, and I thought it would be such a lame thing if my characters weren't half as frank as my uncles.

HILTON ALS

Like one of the *tías* grabbing one of the characters' balls by way of introduction.

JUNOT DÍAZ

I've gotten emails about that from dudes I know, who say, "Dude, my aunts grab my balls, too."

HILTON ALS

It takes a village.

JUNOT DÍAZ

It takes five genders to raise this particularly malevolent form of masculinity that we tend to produce so efficiently. You could take two people, who look identical in skin color, and my mom can distinguish them at the molecular level, and say, "That motherfucker's lighter." All the vocabulary we've lost in America to talk about race is omnipresent in the Caribbean. We've lost so many words to talk about race, we don't even have a conversation about it, we have lost it. Yet, in the Caribbean, there are more than twelve words that I can come up with to describe people's skin color, at least in the neighborhood where I grew up in. In some ways I think that is useful, because it helps when it comes time to approach the question of privilege. People don't claim amnesia. Some can think my uncles are super-backwards because they didn't go to Ivy League schools, but they don't cop to any of that ridiculous liberal amnesia. The sort of thing that translates into statements like, "Oh, it's not race, it's class." I think you can't have class without race. It's called colonialism. Some people come right off the bat and say, a guy is ignorant. My uncles would never make those claims, but rather say it's about black people. But I find that level of frankness, even if it's considered regressive and messed up, a better starting point than the constant illusion of the sort of liberal moment that we have.

HILTON ALS

Is that why the critical discourse around your work hasn't been as substantial as the work itself?

JUNOT DÍAZ

Hilton, that's always weird. It's like talking about—

HILTON ALS

Relatives you haven't met yet.

JUNOT DÍAZ

It's just weird. I have these great cousins, who tell me that I should have better-looking chicks than I do. It's kind of the same thing, a weird statement to make. Like, "I should have better critics than I do."

HILTON ALS

You can have better girls and better critics.

JUNOT DÍAZ

I think for most straight men, the problem is not that we don't have women worthy of us, the problem is that we have women ten times more worthy than us. But coming back to your question, in general, whenever I read about people of color as artists I think it is so overly simplified. We tend to be reduced to the cultural element. Like somebody will trot out a Spanish word to describe our thing . . . How many reviews have I got where a non-Spanish-speaking person will put out a Spanish word to attempt to describe what I do? It's like watching people who can't dance salsa trying to do it. Or we'll be reduced to simplistic visions that say that in these works of art, this artist is talking about this crucial moment, or about the problem of race. They'll use these terms that mean nothing, because they don't want to approach what exactly a person is getting at in their work. If white artists were discussed along racial terms as often as people of color, we would be a better country. I never see a white dancer discussing how their whiteness impacts their dance. The first question out of an interviewer's mind when they talk to a white artist is never if they have experienced racism. But as an artist, I must say it's incredible the amount of times these questions come up, and when they ask me, I'm always ready to ask back, "Have you been racist lately?" Now, one of the best things about art, as anyone who's studied a Victorian text knows, is that the future comes faster than we imagine, and there is a future coming up, of young artists and young critics and young scholars, who are thinking in ways that make the current conversations about our art look incredibly reductive.

HILTON ALS

You touch upon this idea of what's coming up and we've had several conversations about time travel. You've said that one of the reasons why you loved science fiction by people like Octavia Butler and Samuel Delany is because they were talking about time travel, and that literally you have gone from a slave culture to talking to hundreds of people at the Strand Bookstore. How does that happen? Being one or two generations away from the characters in your books, who are living below subsistence level, how does that affect you as Junot?

JUNOT DÍAZ

And how do you narrate it? I always think of that question. I'll sit at the Christmas table next to my grandmother, who basically grew up in a proto-medieval—comes from an almost slavery background in the Dominican Republic, working as a tenant farmer, in a terrifying kind of subsistence. I'm squinting at her with one eye, and then I'm squinting at my little brother, who's U.S.-born, a Marine combat veteran, who sounds like someone turned the TV to the Fox channel and broke the dial. And I'm thinking, how do we create a self that takes both of those people in?

HILTON ALS

You've catapulted yourself, through artistry, into another realm, so how do you physically and emotionally take it?

JUNOT DÍAZ

It's really helpful to assemble selves not always deploying realism. Realism cannot account for my little brother and my grandmother, but Octavia Butler's science fiction can. Samuel Delany's generic experiments can explain them. I read his book and that range is present, not only present, but what is unbearable about trying to hold the two together in one place. So it helps not to have realism as the only paradigm to really understand yourself.

HILTON ALS

Is the story "Monstro" a move towards a surrealism that explains things better?

JUNOT DÍAZ

I wouldn't say it's an advance. It's more a trying to see what would it look like if I was more explicit about not using realism. With *Oscar Wao* I obscured how little the genre of realism is deployed in the novel. I sort of hid it. Someone can read *Oscar Wao* and be convinced it's a realistic novel, with a couple eruptions. Now I wanted to see if it's possible to get similar effects without obscuring the pedigree. I felt like *Oscar Wao* was like an octoroon cousin of yours, who doesn't pass for white, but won't deny it when people treat him real well. I wanted to take the drag off, and see what happens.

HILTON ALS

When you began writing your first fiction, did you know that you were going to focus on your particular world? Was it a process or a discovery? And since you mention that pedigree, I'm wondering why modern writers of color, and Philip Roth, are particularly drawn to that.

JUNOT DÍAZ

I came up as a young activist in college. How many Latinos are here? I don't know if you were part of Latino organizations, like if you had a LALSA, or if you had a LUCHA, or if you had an LAL, or an LAO, or whatever. I was in all. And I was a young activist. That's basically who I was all through college. That was my identity, and in many ways it continues to be my default identity. You know when you wake and you don't know what room you are in or country you are in? The one thing I always know is I'm like, "Fight the man! Get him!" These days they're trying to shut down all the Ethnic Studies programs, because they don't want to produce students who begin by saying, "Yo, it's fucked up we're not talking about us." And I'm a product of these programs that aimed me directly toward writing about this tiny neighborhood that nobody really knew or thought about. It's an old pattern, but one that is super-reliable. We're so erased. If you're a person of color, if you're a woman, if you come from a poor background, if you come from a family who worked like dogs and never got any respect or a share of the profits, you know that ninety percent of your stories ain't told. And yet we still have to be taught to look and to tell our stories. Many of us have to stumble our way through this. Despite the utter absence of us, it's still an internal revolution to say, "Wait a minute. We are not only worthy of great art, but the source of." It takes a lot of work to get there.

HILTON ALS

I'd like you to describe this process. Did you feel that fiction would be the form, or were you writing in other kinds of genres?

JUNOT DÍAZ

I always did fiction and I always wanted to write. When you're young, if you're aware of your parents' infidelities, your cosmology starts with this concept that your parents are real big liars. My cosmology begins with this constant deception. So of course I wanted to write about deceivers, people who were wearing masks, and for this purpose fiction felt more useful. As a kid I was that literal, thinking I lived in fiction, so let me write it. It started there, and it seems it's going to end there. I was always terrible with essays, whether they are confessional or critical, because in that form the whole thing can't be a lie. My idea for an essay would be to write about a book that's never been written, or to draw a completely ridiculous conclusion, and then when somebody checks the footnotes . . . I think in fiction, I can lie on multiple levels, which is always what my family felt like. I felt at home.

HILTON ALS

That essay sounds Borgesian. But looking at your first collection, were there stories that were just a sort of working out before you got *Drown*?

JUNOT DÍAZ

Certainly, I had so many absurd stories. I still hadn't mapped out what it meant to be living in central New Jersey. We were one of the first Dominican families in the area and we grew up around a predominantly African-American community, with some poor whites, most of them Irish immigrants. I couldn't figure out how to scale a family that existed in this really dense Dominican world at home. I had siblings who were black, who didn't look like me, who weren't, like, Terrorism Act bait. They looked African-American and I couldn't figure out a way to scale it. I was reading so many New York writers describing the Latino experience in a really urban setting that my first stories sounded like I was living in NYC, which is a very different world.

HILTON ALS

Who were you reading?

JUNOT DÍAZ

People like Edward Rivera, who wrote *Family Installments*, probably one of the greatest memoirs. If you want to know how I wrote my first book, read that, because I just completely copied that book. I also read some of the most classic folks, such as Nicholasa Mohr—even though she was writing about Paterson, it still had a much more urban edge—or Piri Thomas. In my first thirty or forty pieces of writing, a character was always robbing a bodega. It was so stupid. I was an embarrassment to myself. I started out writing film scripts, and before, you know, I jumped to fiction, but even then, I wanted to do a kind of film scripts. So my first few years I was doing scripts, and those were even worse than anything anyone can imagine.

HILTON ALS

When did you find your voice? When do you feel that you made something good enough to be sent out, to be published?

JUNOT DÍAZ

I never feel that, but I do remember finding my voice while I was writing a page that got thrown out of *Drown*. That was the guiding spirit of it, and it'll go back in if I ever write another book . . . You know how everybody today wants to claim urban backgrounds? If you look at fashion and compare a bunch of pictures of what women wore back in 1992 and how they dress now, you can see how these clothes and looks have been completely Latinized. All women are dressing now like Latinas. For real. Don't make me bring the slide projector out.

HILTON ALS

There's this great quote of Capote, in an interview by Warhol. He said he really liked Bianca Jagger, because she was South American chic. Warhol asked what was that, and Capote says that it's a Spanish adaptation of Negro culture.

JUNOT DÍAZ

How about a Spanish *continuation* of Negro culture? Because most of the cultures we're talking about were deeply Africanized. But going back to that one page I mentioned before, I remembered every time we would have to visit my family in the Bronx or in East New York, my siblings would beg not to go. You couldn't go outside. People would always menace us when we would go to the store. And I remember writing that page, and realizing that this was so different from that memoir *Fresh Off the Boat.*

What I want to point out is that there's been this whole tendency where everybody wants to take on this hip urban culture. As a kid I remember it and we were already part of that culture, and we didn't want to get stuck in the Bronx. We were so honest that at eleven and twelve, we were sure we did not want to go up there. Then as soon as I had that scene written down, I knew I had nailed my New Jersey moment, where we were black and Latino. There were no identity issues about that we weren't or were, but we didn't want to go to East New York, and we were honest.

HILTON ALS

I didn't want to go there, either, and I grew up there.

JUNOT DÍAZ

You grew up there! You know the deal.

HILTON ALS

One of the things that beats beautifully in *Drown* and all your work goes back to this idea that if you're an artist, the hardest thing to survive is the people you come from. And the people that you come from are the stories that you tell. Often. Can you tell us a little bit about your family reaction?

JUNOT DÍAZ

That is a really honest question and recognition. Most of my friends had to protect their parents and the rest of us from their ambitions. A childhood like mine meant that you could not openly air your ambitions to people because it would have been an enormous threat. When I think about it, I guess my family's situation was always a heartbreaker, regardless how my career turned out. The family dynamic internalized all the craziness of growing up as an immigrant. Immigration is difficult as it is, but the worst way to take it on the chin is to turn it against each other.

HILTON ALS

Right.

JUNOT DÍAZ

It's weird, my immediate family gets together almost never, and when we get together, it's always like a heartbreaker. There's all this kind of awful stuff: who's not talking to whom, how some brothers live in California, as far away from the family as possible. And I'll be honest, I think my family barely tolerates me, and part of the barely-tolerates-me is that I should never speak about my art, that's like the price of admission. If I want to go home and sit through Christmas dinner and not have a meltdown, I should never ever talk about it. I'll lie. I'm a big old coward, not a complete coward. Because no matter who you are, you can stand up to a whole bunch of different stuff, but sometimes it's really hard. I'm still auditioning for my family's love. I still hold out this thing that they'll be nicer if I play along. You wrestle with your family your entire life. People who don't, that's like the most blessed resource in the world, since the rest of us are still caught in a dynamic which doesn't always leave too much room for you to be compassionate to yourself.

HILTON ALS

While that narrative is going on, and it's deeply painful, you are able to be open enough and funny enough and friendly enough to find someone like me, who was not so different. We can make our own family. That's a declaration of love.

JUNOT DÍAZ

Those of us who have near misses with families yearn for families. I grew up around Koreans, and let me tell you something, if you know anything about that national history it's like the Caribbean in a day, compressed madness. But you'd meet people whose families are the only reason they survived from starvation, and you get the sense that it can really work, though there are other relationships, too, that can do the same thing. I'm just arguing that, when it works, it has some strength. So, of course, I'm a kid who's always looking for people that I can connect with profoundly, and I'm willing to take the risk. You get kicked around enough, and you either do two things: you withdraw totally, or you say, I can take another kick.

HILTON ALS

Can I share the jokes we told each other about fathers this Christmas? My favorite was, Junot said, "Yo, your father was like my father. He would drive by the house in his car and that was a visit." It was really true. Except my father didn't have the car.

JUNOT DÍAZ

Right. Yeah. Again, it's a Jersey thing. With no train, they start saving for their cars when they're nine.

HILTON ALS

Do you think that part of the struggle, all worth it for *Oscar Wao*, was learning how to become a public figure while you were involved in this private occupation of writing?

JUNOT DÍAZ

Oh, no. I wrote my first book, and the sales would convince you not to be a writer, but it got some notoriety among people who were into fiction, among public school teachers, Dominicans, and allies, such as the Puerto Rican, the Cuban, the Chicano community, but that was it. I wrote this book in 1996, and I spent the next eleven years having like no career. I had a six-year period where I didn't even publish like a minor essay. It was awesome. I got this little burst of attention, then I proceeded to lose . . .

When I hear my students talking, they have all this professional language. They are all ready to be famous; they use words like *momentum*. So part of the experience of *Oscar Wao* was out-waiting my desire to sound like my students. I didn't want to hear myself saying, "You've gotta publish this fast, you've got momentum. Strike while people know who you are." I remember spending at least five years just waiting for that voice to die, for real. I didn't write anything useful until that voice died, till it no longer had control of the board. When I finally heard the voice say, "Well, you should just write the bad book that you *knew* you were going to write, because you *suck*," I was like *go*. It took sixteen years for *This Is How You Lose Her* to get done. I had to keep wrestling with that voice. I had to wait for the moments that voice died, so I could write the next chapter. If it would flare up again I wouldn't be able to work on the book.

HILTON ALS

There are other voices that intrude into your life in beautiful ways. I remember one day we were walking down Sixth Avenue, and all of a sudden I heard three girls screaming, "Junot!" One of them said she had been waiting for your new book. Can you take that voice?

JUNOT DÍAZ

Nah. Because the engine that propels me is the one that doesn't want to be anybody's friend, doesn't want popularity. I'm not joking. I'm not that bad a writer. I can write a short story collection in under sixteen years. You may trust me when I tell you there's nothing wrong with my "craft," it's just that none of those other voices produce the horrifying deceptive intimacy that I need to tell my stories. There has to be this voice, there has to be a presence in the book that wants to tell the truth . . .

I grew up in a post-dictatorship dictatorship society. The axis of likability is how dictatorships survive. Becoming popular is part of what dictatorships hijack to remain in power. For me to write things from the same toxic axis that made stronger the dictatorship that completely disfigured my family and my society, it just wasn't going to happen. My father was a Dominican military police apparatchik. He was emblematic of that culture. And I lived in a place where it was so much better to be liked because your shirt was ironed, or because you had a good posture. It was just insane, the way a military dictatorship is like Reddit. Honestly, man.

HILTON ALS

Something like *The Autumn of the Patriarch* by Gabriel García Márquez is a work of realism.

JUNOT DÍAZ

Autumn of the Patriarch takes the twilight of it. My experience of living in a post-dictatorship society is that everybody believes that they're going to be the Reddit article that gets pushed all the way up. The like axis is just very, very powerful, and I needed to tilt a different way. I needed to say that it is possible to say things, to be involved in a conversation with people where the relationship is determined by things more complicated than whether you like me or not. Maybe the content of my communication would be in itself worthy of discussion, regardless of how you felt at an emotional level about the person bringing the news. In a dictatorship, the two things get quickly put together. The news you bring stands as a moral judgment about you, and this is the way you keep critics silent, because you basically say, "If you criticize the dictatorship, it's not only your thinking, your *body* is out of order, which is why we must destroy your body."

HILTON ALS

So this writing is an act of defiance.

JUNOT DÍAZ

This is how I understand it. This is like a self-aggrandizing lunacy that helps me understand why I wait so long, and why I hear that voice so clearly. I'm so desirous to want to play along with that, with my father. I knew that if I ironed my clothes every day, my dad would like me, but my dad made a mistake and took me to the military prisons in the Dominican Republic that he worked in. His game was to put us in the cells, pretend to lock the doors, and walk away. My brother thought this was the funniest thing, but I remember looking around at the feces-covered walls and thinking, we were in the space of this culture. Even though I didn't have the language to express it then, I knew that this was home. My dad was taking me to work, but he was also taking me home. That created in me a deep visceral desire to tack a different way, because that's not where I wanted to end up. Despite the fact that I would have loved to set up a torture-prison if my dad would have loved me, I was trying to figure out how even with that impulse, how could I pull away?

HILTON ALS

How did you build your own home?

JUNOT DÍAZ

I think part of it is what you identified. It's hard to describe my family without seeming completely made up, but what got you love was how many fights you won in the leisurely arranged boxing matches in our neighborhood, and how many bullets you nailed to the target during our Saturday rifle-range outing. My escape from that weird regime was trying to read. Being a nerd was an act of escape in my family, because everything else was like, shoot guns and get punched by your neighbors.

HILTON ALS

Reading as an act of aggression and salvation; parents who don't read, who don't have any access to that stuff, often think that a child is putting up a wall. And they're not agreeing with them. But they can't say it's wrong.

JUNOT DÍAZ

They're so caught in the enlightenment bind. Your parents, especially if they're immigrants, know that the only way out is education. At the same time, when my family would see me with a book, they would be like, "¡Anormal! Go outside and play!" There was this constant back-and-forth, and as a kid you find spaces there where at least you can hide.

Questions from the Audience

This question has to do with This Is How You Lose Her. *We read it for one of my classes, and one of the topics of discussion was why you included the chapter with the women who work at the Laundromat.*

JUNOT DÍAZ

Wait a minute, are you doing a paper? Just checking. I know this sounds completely ridiculous, but the persona who writes my books, is a writer writing my books, Yunior, is a big liar, and he filters the whole thing. He's also way smarter than I am, because one can write someone who is smarter than you. One of the things about Yunior is that he *loves* to destabilize a reader's sense of who he is and who his family is, and he loves breaking up any kind of authoritative narrative about his family or himself. So he will actually tell different versions of a story. In my first book, *Drown*, you have a version of the story, where his father abandons the family, and goes and lives in the United States, a story called "Negocios." This is a second iteration of the story, told from the point of view of the woman whom his father almost leaves the family for. He keeps the father's name, but changes everything around, because this way it's hard to tell which story is true. Yunior is so not about truth.

It's not just something that's to make up stuff. In *Drown*, the first book, you see Yunior describe his brother and his brother's relationship in great detail and then stop talking about it, there is complete silence about where the brother goes. In *This Is How You Lose Her*, you realize that the brother has died of cancer, and that the brother had been dead of cancer in the first book, but it had been completely left out. I always assumed this second book would come, and it would explain the first, but it would also destabilize it. So that particular story about the Laundromat is Yunior retelling what would be called "his family's foundational myth." If I ever write my next book in this series, Yunior will tell that story again. For those of us who grew up in immigrant families, the foundational story takes on this luminous glow. It takes on its own authority, except it's completely fictitious, because, if you pay attention, the story doesn't ever cohere. There's always stuff that doesn't come together. People always switch their narratives.

As a fiction writer, did you ever worry about misrepresenting the immigrant experience?

JUNOT DÍAZ

No. People want to read stories by "marginal artists" as universal in the exact wrong way we want them to be read. I want to be read as universal not because this stands in for all Dominicans and therefore this is a great map for any of you who are going to that country. This story is about one tiny dot in that shifting constellation of people and moments and identities that we would call the Dominican diaspora. I'm not claiming to represent anyone but this tiny group of people. I mean, why do you think I'd create a character like Oscar, who absolutely fits no formula of what is a Dominican? He spends his whole time saying he really is Dominican while everybody insists on saying he is not.

All art, because it scales to the human, because of that human-level distortion, is disqualified from becoming a stand-in for a nation, or a time. There's something about the granular complexity of any novel, or short story collection, which almost seems to immediately invalidate it as a larger argument about this group or this people. If you understand that complexity, you shouldn't get worried. I think that we only worry about this because we ourselves sometimes want to claim partially that we're spokespeople for our nation. Por abajo, on the lower frequencies, where we don't like to admit things, we really truly want to be the writer of our generation, of our people, of our moment. That's what leads us all astray. On the one hand, we don't want to be called out for that, but on the other hand, we want all the banners and prizes and privileges that come with that. It's a terrible, terrible two-headed dragon to serve.

You describe this childhood of deprivation, and this experience of growing up with crazy role models. How do you explain the fact that you succeeded so beautifully, and didn't succumb to all the other terrible things that could have happened to you and follow these dysfunctional paths?

JUNOT DÍAZ

But who says I haven't? I'm not just being tendentious. This is the mythography of America, progressive, where you have this idea that everything moves upward, and people are always on this journey to improvement. So, "How did you make it?" Listen, this is very important to understand, I don't speak the language of "make it." Our moment, in late capital, has no problems, through its contradictions, occasionally granting someone ridiculous moments of privilege, but that's not what matters. In other words, we can elect Obama, but what does that say about the fate of the African-American community? We have no problem in this country rewarding individuals of color momentarily as a way never to address structural cannibalistic inequalities that are faced by the communities these people come out of.

And the record ain't done yet. Has anybody tabulated my full account of cruelties towards people? I just mean . . . I don't think we can safely say just because someone has some sort of visible markers of success that in any way they have avoided any of the dysfunctions. That is the kind of Chaucerian, weird physiognomy-as-moral-status. We don't know anything about anybody. Yes, I have made a certain level of status as an artist and as a writer, but what I am reminded of most acutely is not of my "awesomeness," or some sort of will to power that has led me through the jungle. What I am aware of, being here, is that I am representative of a structural exclusion.

I'm sure you felt some sort of displacement within your society and especially in your own culture. How did you overcome that?

JUNOT DÍAZ

I think we accept too much at face value these ideologies of transcendence, that one overcomes their . . . I guess my first thing was that I noticed *nobody* was at home. I think that some of us have better operational masquerades than others. Last time I noticed, America isn't epically addicted to cocaine, especially white upper-middle-class America, because it feels at home, because it feels comfortable in its own skin. Some of our displacements are pathologized in ways that other people's displacements are. We try to explain everything is that we're immigrants of color. Because that's the way the society explains everything, it's the easy go-to myth. But I just knew, from everything that I saw, that there is no transcending the human experience. You've got to realize that most of us feel permanently displaced and savagely undone. Most of us try everything we can to manage our fears and our insecurities. Most of us are profoundly inhuman to ourselves and other people, and that makes us no less valuable, and no less worthy of attention and love. I didn't transcend all this stuff, you just got to live with them, man, and there's nothing like trying to run away from all that stuff to guarantee its supremacy. My idea is to change at least the percentage of the vote. These voices are always going to get a vote, but do they always have to have the majority of the vote?

HILTON ALS

They don't get to win all the time.

JUNOT DÍAZ

You try to distribute who you are in different proportions, but the transcendence myth will just do you in, in the long run.

HILTON ALS

And this idea of the arrival myth is what you're speaking of, that once we arrive . . . but one of the great and amazing things about America and Americans is that they never do.

JUNOT DÍAZ

No. Only one person attended my first reading at Boston, my best friend, Shuya Ohno. Today, there are all these fine faces here, but tomorrow, you're back to one person. America is not like Latin America, that tends to be much more committed to its artists, and you could be thirty years in the game and not publish one book and people still think you matter. We are a fickle, fickle nation, and today's arrival is tomorrow's "See, I told you, what a fraud." Somebody will come along and that's the reality of it. I know that I'm back to reading to my boy Shuya, always in my heart, because that's the place where most of us end up as artists, and you have to be comfortable there, no matter what your fantasies of supremacy and success are, because tomorrow that's where you'll be at.

The best part about art is that as long as the civilization survives, somebody out there will keep one copy of your text, and perhaps that will give comfort, inspiration, and more importantly a space for an individual to be in touch with their humanity. To be temporarily in touch with their best selves, which is fragile, flawed, weak, scared . . . That's worth working, and that's the moment why most of us go this very long, shadowed path into producing art, because we fundamentally believe that what we do is the best of what we call human, the best of us, even if at times we don't like to recognize it.

3

Rivka Galchen, Hari Kunzru, & Rachel Kushner

WITH MÓNICA DE LA TORRE

MÓNICA DE LA TORRE

I wanted to start by asking you about your experience of temporal shifts in the writing process. Can you speak about your work when it's in the incubation process?

HARI KUNZRU

At the moment, I'm doing some screenwriting, and you're forced to talk about everything all the time with people who don't seem to share very much with you. And so you're always trying to reach your idea across a table. There seems to be an increasing amount of that in the fiction-publishing industry as well. I started something, and was kind of happy to talk about it, but I am now feeling that I hollowed it out in some way by doing that. Now I started something else and I'm not talking about that, and it feels good, it feels precious.

MÓNICA DE LA TORRE

You'd rather not to talk about something that's in its early stages because you feel that you might jinx it?

HARI KUNZRU

A novel certainly takes so long that it has to be a project that you can live inside for a period of years, at least a couple. It has to be a machine that can somehow process all of your stuff, your experiences during that time, even if it's in a very oblique and coded way. I think with oversharing you risk that it doesn't function. I'm quite interested in privacy.

RACHEL KUSHNER

After you finish a book for a publisher you're still inside a pretty endless process of copyediting and proofreading, etc. So I feel like I was with *Flamethrowers* in a continual way basically until it came out, at which point I had to begin to talk about it. You have to create a sort of discourse that then you utilize over and over again, as you're asked questions. But that only happens through experience. Having done it before for a first book didn't at all prepare me for the second. Writers construct in writing. It's hard to improvise. With a book, even though all of the ideas in the book are mine, and I had total control over the novel, there are so many different things that go into writing a novel at different moments, and the temporality of it is protracted, the writing of it. When it's time to give an encapsulation of all your different thematic interests and the materials that were important to the book, I forget sometimes what inspired me. I have to make cheat sheets. Eventually you learn how to talk about your own book, but the frightening thing about this is that then you can go on autopilot. Right now I'm on a book tour and I feel like I could accidentally sell myself a pair of overpriced shoes or something.

HARI KUNZRU

Isn't that the purpose of the book tour? To alienate you so much from the thing that you've written that you feel forced to write something else, in order to feel good about yourself again?

RACHEL KUSHNER

When I talk about a book, it's already long written and I've already moved on to the next, which I wouldn't talk about. I've looked at what other novelists have done, and I read authors saying, "I'm not talking about that." It's either because it's bad luck, or it deflates some of the penumbra or whatever of the idea to leak it out. I don't know if that's the reason why I don't.

RIVKA GALCHEN

Often it seems like you're choosing between being true and accurate to what you're doing, and being a nice person, answering people's questions. It's a tension. I imagine you start feeling like you have a bit of a shtick, but the shtick is the friendly thing to do. So, it's a little bit of a bind.

HARI KUNZRU

I really admire writers who cannot go along with that. I'm dreadfully prone to taking whatever stupid question it is, and trying to make something out of it. You end up feeling terrible.

MÓNICA DE LA TORRE

My next question is about repurposing skills that you've learned in other environments, in order perhaps to add realism to a novel. For instance, Rachel, you are also an art critic and your descriptions in *Flamethrowers*, not only of artworks, but also of particular scenes, are so realistic and so believable that I often found myself wondering if it wasn't a roman à clef. I wondered if you weren't disguising actual artists under different names. Maybe you've done it, too, Hari, you were a music editor, you wrote about technology. In your case, Rivka, you're an M.D. in psychiatry. So, I wanted to ask you all, is it deliberate that you bring those skills to the novel? Does it feel slightly subversive, perhaps, that you're taking what belongs in the realm of your day job and bringing it into the realm of fiction?

HARI KUNZRU

I wanted to be a fiction writer before I wanted to do anything else, like write journalism. It was very accidental that I wrote about technology. At a certain point, in my early twenties, it turned out that my only marketable skill was knowing about the Internet. I was working for *Wired* at the point when it was a sort of Day-Glo-orange cult based in San Francisco. They would send me off to talk to people who would tell me that the future was being physically instantiated somewhere in the Valley, these extraordinary characters, who were very alien to my way of thinking. I remember asking my boss that we were always writing about these wealthy people who are making the future, or so they told us, but what about everybody else? I was told very sternly that there are no have-nots, only have-laters. I realized that everybody was insane, and I needed to write a novel about it. I was given a lot of material from that, by accident, really, but there's a fairly easy flow for me across the boundaries between fiction and nonfiction. I like doing journalism partly because it gets me out of the house. It's quite a relief not to be inside my head. And, yes, you get a little window onto other kinds of life.

RACHEL KUSHNER

Every writer is different, but for me the novel is a challenge that requires every single part of myself. Therefore, every single thing that I know about the world is going to be summoned in some way by whatever I'm working on. I think a lot of writers are like that, and I think across genre, too. It's like Anne Carson, by no accident, will write about Monica Vitti, or about Sappho. Well, she's a classicist, not that Monica Vitti has to do with classicism. But I was just thinking about different things she's interested in and that she'll incorporate into her poetry. I'm not at all comparing myself with Anne Carson, she's legitimately a classicist; I am not legitimately anything, really, except for a fiction writer. I do write about art on occasion, and have done so for many years now, but I don't really consider myself an art critic, like a taste-maker type of person, and nor am I an art historian, because I'm not trained that way. Still, I'm interested in contemporary art and culture, it's a knowledge that I got in a semi-autodidactic but organic fashion, after having been assigned various pieces.

When it came time to write this novel, it was no accident that I wanted to write a book that was partly set in the art world of downtown New York in the seventies. It was something that I'd picked up a few ideas about just along the way. But it's definitely not a roman à clef. The characters are fictional, entirely constructed. I do like the cameo, it's fun to place a real person in a scene—like John Chamberlain, drunkenly moving through the room. It could just give a tiny reminder for the reader that they're in a real space.

But I tried to downplay the art world in *Flamethrowers*. I don't like to read novels about the art world where there are long descriptions about the character's conceptual artwork. You can tell that the writer is making it up and kind of getting lost inside of the writing of the fictional stuff that the character makes. It comes across to me as precious. So I just tried to signify that these people make works, but did not go too in-depth into what they made. For me, part of the great fun and the challenge is that writing summons everything you know. Still, you do not want to be a Little Miss Know-It-All.

RIVKA GALCHEN

What were some of the images that were important to you while you were working?

RACHEL KUSHNER

I collected a lot of images while I was working on *Flamethrowers*. The book is about the seventies, but I'm also interested in futurism and its relationship to war, and I'm interested in motorcycles and technology and the way that speed was introduced via war. One of the first images that I put up was of a soldier from World War I riding a motorcycle with a really crazy sidecar contraption on it that was shaped like a bullet. There was another guy in the sidecar who looked like he was kind of his amanuensis. He had a typing machine and was taking notes. That sounds kind of precious! I found the picture online and just put it up in my office. I did that with several others. The image that's on the cover of my book was another one. You can print things out on a black-and-white printer and it somehow looks okay. I had all kinds of images up on the wall while I was writing. Stills from films, like the last by Guy Debord, *In girum imus nochte et consumimur igni*, with all of those different pictures that he used, and the subtitle comments that he made over the images. That right there is a kind of crystallization of language and image that he put together. Debord was a real master at combining words and images. A lot of that film is just still after still, with his commentary over it.

There's a whole range of things that I worked with. Sometimes an image for me is just an image in my mind. For example, I was thinking about the blackout in New York City in 1977, and the hostility in the press to the looting and criminality that went on. Then I was thinking about a march in Rome earlier that year, on March 12th, 1977. I thought about crowds that fill up the street, following a certain logic, but in an unexpected manner. In New York no one knew that the electricity was going to go off, and in Rome no one knew a student was going to be killed by the police in Bologna the day before, which is what precipitated the outpouring of people to the streets, who came from all over Italy. I thought about those two events, and to me those were images, in a way. They have some similarity.

HARI KUNZRU

I often have several things that I know go together, but don't rationally go together. For example, in my last novel I did not know why computer modeling and the stock market should have anything to do with the Mojave Desert, but they had. I then had to write to find out what that connection was.

RACHEL KUSHNER

Did you look at images while you were writing about those cult followers who lived in the desert?

HARI KUNZRU

There's a good book called *Spaced Out*. It's about utopian architecture in the 1960s, and it has a lot of visual references to western United States communes. I also have a friend in San Francisco whose art practice revolves around that, so she's always finding things online and sending me pictures of people at Morning Star, looking like they hadn't had a bath.

RACHEL KUSHNER

Did you print them out, too, and put them up in your office?

HARI KUNZRU

I'm trying to remember what I had up at that point. I've moved around a lot in the last few years, but I definitely had that thing of papering my walls with my sort of projection of my book. Now, for the last two years the only thing I've had up in my writing space—it's a sort of gag—is one of Mao's speeches. It's published as a Peking Press pamphlet with the cream covers, and it's called "Oppose Book Worship." It just says "oppose book worship" above my screen. And that feels like a useful thing to remind myself.

RIVKA GALCHEN

I wonder about this methodology of not really being in control, where you have a couple of interests that just seem to sit on the surgical table together, whatever it is, the sewing machine and the umbrella. What is that like in the composition process? It sounds like both of you feel most in control if you are not in control. If you don't know why you're interested in Italy in the seventies and New York in the seventies, or machines, what does that make your daily process like?

RACHEL KUSHNER

To me, the work of the novel is to not be in control, and to be moving at a patient pace towards a future that is not a foregone conclusion. I want there to be a certain quotient of mystery always, when I'm writing. Maybe halfway through the book I know how it's going to end, and it's a matter of getting there, but there are still things that are going to happen that I haven't foreseen. For me, the process of the novel and the challenge of it is partly to figure out how these two realms are related. I did not want things to overrelate in a very reducible, clean, and very symphonic way. Like, "Oh, it turns out that she's the cousin of the man who . . ." I don't mean to denigrate that, but it's not my style as a thinker or reader or writer. I want things to be more open, and to think about cities, and history, and events, and have one person who kind of just moves through these landscapes. I wanted the registration of how they echo one another to take place in the mind of the reader, not so much in the page.

For me it's just time, too. You have a few years to figure these things out. I'll work on one small part, and then another. It's like moving tanks to the front lines. You can't get there in one day when you're moving provisions.

HARI KUNZRU

I like the image of you as General Rommel.

RACHEL KUSHNER

But it is like that! The blackout in New York and the march in Italy in 1977 were two crowd scenes, it was a set of images around which some ideas revolved, and then it resulted in this novel. I recently visited the rare book and manuscript library at Yale, the Beinecke Library. There is a curator there who has collected every bit of ephemera from the autonomous movement in Italy that he could find, and he put out all of these papers. At the end of one of the tables was this enormous broadsheet that these people in Italy had made of the blackout in New York City. It had King Kong on top of the Empire State Building, and all of these epithets in Italian reveling in the criminality of this one night in New York. I've kept asking myself about the similarities between these two events and it was all right there, in this one image. That felt kind of vindicating, it goes back to Rivka's question about the many years where you don't really know how two things are related.

HARI KUNZRU

When I was digging around in the seventies political ephemera in London, I went to the British Library. What they had, had largely been stolen or had been badly defaced. Nobody was paying any attention to this. I ended up having a lot more luck with eBay than I did with libraries. Nobody wants to read tedious Maoist tracts from 1973 other than me, and it was a great work-displacement activity as well. I'm actually working, but I'm really into this eBay auction. Now I have a little collection that I made myself. I should probably donate it.

RACHEL KUSHNER

But that is work, too, don't you think? You're doing something for the book, like you're giving glow or mystification to the lost.

HARI KUNZRU

There was something about handling these materials that felt important. I also felt I was betraying them in a certain way. Because, of course, when you are treating these things as a collector you're absolutely defusing them of any kind of the political importance that its authors had hoped that they would have. So, actually, you're right. It was quite useful, while I was writing, to think about my own impulses around these materials.

RACHEL KUSHNER

How did you get interested in King Mob initially?

HARI KUNZRU

King Mob was a sort of offshoot of the Situationist International—there were a bunch of people in West London, around Notting Hill, in the late sixties, early seventies, who had contact with the SI and with the Up Against the Wall Motherfucker people here in New York. In fact, I think they were kicked out of the SI because they supported the Motherfuckers in a row with Raoul Vaneigem. There were these two brothers called the Wise brothers, who were at the center of King Mob.

There was a piece of graffiti that lasted from whenever they did it, sometime around the 1970s, until well into the 1990s. That's how I first knew about the group. There was this huge long wall that went round by the Tube line as you were going towards Ladbroke Grove, overground, on the Overland, and it said, "Same thing day after day—tube—work—dinner—work—tube—armchair—TV—sleep—tube—work—how much more can you take? One in ten go mad, one in five crack up." As a kid I would always wonder, what's the difference between going mad and cracking up? This graffiti was part of my childhood life. Then I realized that these guys had done it, and that it was part of this campaign that they had of writing slogans up, Poetry will be made by all, not by one. That sort of thing.

As an adult I fell into this milieu in London where there were the sort of remnants of SI-affiliated things and various kinds of currents of utopian anarchism. There were these people called the Association of Autonomous Astronauts who I used to know. They thought that space travel should be for all and that we should start making a bottom-up plan to go to space. There were meetings and publications, and people would give papers on how we might get to space and what we might do in space if we got there. Would we have a rave? Would we have sex? What were the possibilities of space? I did not realize at the time, but all of these people were part of this tradition that led back to King Mob and beyond.

MÓNICA DE LA TORRE

If writing a novel is slowly moving the trucks toward the frontline, what is writing a short story like? I am curious about Rivka's process, because you've written a novel and now you're writing short stories.

RIVKA GALCHEN

The trucks thing is nice. I always forget that "avant-garde" is a military term, which isn't an accident. You always have to call up some enemies to make sure there's someone to meet you on the other side. I think of the same analogy but from the other side. Maybe something about short story writing puts you in a smaller state of mind. I think of it as if you're trying to grow mushrooms, but you can't plant mushrooms. Still, you want to grow them. That's how I feel about the short story process: You know that if you came up with it, it can't be that good, because it fits in your head. You hope that it can be like sprout, a little bit on paper, or with the help of time and paper and chance intersection with old interests you didn't know you have, or old memories that pop up. This involves a lot of waiting. Because there are no seeds to plant, you have to wait for some spore to show up, and then think about what kind of temperature would make it slightly more interested in landing. I'm not sure that's so different from a novel, or it wasn't for me.

MÓNICA DE LA TORRE

It would seem that at some point you do have a sense of direction in a novel. What you're describing seems to be the opposite. You distrust a sense of direction.

RIVKA GALCHEN

A novel is so big that the possible ways keep shrinking. With the first word you still have like a bazillion words that might be the second word, but by the time you're on the thirty-five thousandth word there are only like a million words that might be the next one. It just starts to contract a little bit.

HARI KUNZRU

It's a very melancholic part of writing a novel, isn't it? At the beginning you have an almost infinite sense of how great this thing is going to be, and then it narrows down to what you've actually done.

RACHEL KUSHNER

To me, there's a kind of horror in the infinite.

HARI KUNZRU

Have you ever had writer's block, felt some panic when confronting the blank page?

RACHEL KUSHNER

I hear about that a lot. The blank page. I don't know if I've ever had writer's block or not. That's sort of like, "Am I a neurotic or just a normal human being?"

When I start a book, that infinite possibility is more challenging. You think you can just include everything, but then you can't. Once I know what I'm doing, it's much more pleasurable.

HARI KUNZRU

Is that what happened to you with *Telex from Cuba*? The amount of research you did was insane, wasn't it? You worked for years.

RACHEL KUSHNER

I did. It was my first novel, it was a learning process, and I did a lot of research because it was a time and a place I didn't know anything about. Everything had happened before I was born and in a place I'd never lived. I felt I had to metabolize the whole long baroque history of Cuban politics leading up to and through the revolution, in order to be able to write. Now I don't do things that way anymore. I didn't do any research for my new book because I was writing about realms that I felt I had some kind of handle on, which is why I chose to move towards them. Still, there was a full array of possibilities. I get an idea, there's a set of things that could happen, and then as I start to write it's the narrative itself that closes down the other possibilities. But the closing down for me is very reassuring, because once I'm on a specific track, and I know who the characters are, and what kinds of things I want to happen, I have a much better sense of what I'm doing. I want to get to a point where I'm writing sentences that can reassure the reader that they're in good hands, and until I'm to that point I'm just not sure. Things could open out and open out, and I don't want the novel to be arbitrary. That's the thing. And, as a reader, I don't like it when I encounter something that seems arbitrary to me. So that's my fantasy—to create a book that doesn't have any arbitrary components.

HARI KUNZRU

As a reader I, too, have a problem with certain sorts of absurdism and postmodernism, where you realize that the next thing could be completely arbitrary. My interest drains away at that point, even if in an abstract, intellectual way I admire the structure that is being proposed.

RIVKA GALCHEN

You want that mix where it feels like a surprise, hopefully even to the writer, and inevitable. You want a logic, even if you want it to be complicated enough that you couldn't have seen through to the end of it. It's that *Alice in Wonderland* thing, where you think every turn seems very unexpected, and absolutely logical. Like it couldn't have been something else.

MÓNICA DE LA TORRE

This reminds me of something that César Aira talks about when he describes his writing process. He goes forward and is open to arbitrary occurrences. Anything random is likely to be included in the novel.

RACHEL KUSHNER

He's way more productive than anyone sitting up here.

MÓNICA DE LA TORRE

He's written like a hundred books, if not more.

RIVKA GALCHEN

He is describing a methodology, not a product. He's written plenty of books and some of them are amazing and some of them are slightly less amazing. But I feel that's a bit like jazz. There is a methodology with a deep logic running through it, and it's using the fuel of chance in order to push itself. In a sense, the product is not arbitrary because the method is so rigorous.

HARI KUNZRU

It's not totally dissimilar to Raymond Roussel making a method out of puns, and then forcing the story on through that.

RACHEL KUSHNER

It's also like those painters, a sort of old-fashioned AbEx modality where they say, "You know, I just throw something up on the canvas, and then I respond, and then I put something else up on the canvas, and I respond to that." I'm not belittling that. But there are so many ways of making a painting, right? It's the end product really that matters. You can bring the same kind of process to every single painting and end up with different results.

HARI KUNZRU

I saw a Gutai show at the Guggenheim and it's exactly that. They're attempting not to control the materials. One guy is painting with his feet because he has less control. Other people are using drips and responding in various ways to the kinds of materials that they're using, that they can only kind of nudge rather than completely control top-down.

MÓNICA DE LA TORRE

You're ventriloquizing an AbEx painter. Some people even refer to that as ventriloquism in a way. It's like this dialogue with the material. You're throwing your voice onto this thing that you're creating, and it speaks back to you, and tells you what it needs.

HARI KUNZRU

That's like when writers say that their characters just started talking.

RACHEL KUSHNER

Yes, that's shit.

Cheever were amazing writers. Of course they were, but because I knew they were, or I knew that I was supposed to really get excited by them, they were at the bottom. I got accidentally tricked into reading them.

HARI KUNZRU

My wife is also a novelist, Katie Kitamura. She has recently taken to saying that her idea for her prose is to make it sound as if it's been translated out of something else into English.

RIVKA GALCHEN

That's the dream, of writing like Aleksandar Hemon. You just think, "Why is English my first language? What a curse!" It is a great constraint for every word to be off-key a little bit.

HARI KUNZRU

But that sort of ambition to make language strange, which is clearly at the core of every artistic use of language—that's something to do with that. Aleksandar Hemon clearly has that, in a very direct way in those early stories before his English was absolutely spot-on, he accidentally made the language new. There's this sort of uncanny quality, there's a flatness that comes with a certain sort of tone that a translated piece sometimes has, something that's not there on the page that you're stretching towards. And that's quite an interesting tone in itself—the gap between what's there and the possibly completely imagined hinterland to that language. The flatter it is on the surface the weirder it is, too.

RACHEL KUSHNER

Another reason I read a lot of writers who don't write originally in English is because I sort of want to educate myself under the spirit of a conversation that (and I hate to say it) is taking place in Europe. It starts with Baudelaire, or even before him, with Chateaubriand, and then Benjamin takes them all up and kind of theorizes about them. Sartre and Deleuze write beautifully about these people. There are all of these French writers that are part of a bigger conversation that's partly taking place not just between writers, but among their critical and philosophical champions. I'm interested to know what Lacan was reading, and he incorporates certain people into his lectures. That to me is sort of like a mysterious world. For me it's less about language being translated than about these people being part of a kind of world that I imagine, I want to learn more about, and I pursue.

HARI KUNZRU

There is a danger in the nostalgia for the twentieth century avant-garde, though, isn't there? There's a lot of avant-garde posturing that goes on and it's not functional now. I am interested in that feeling of belatedness that a lot of writers, especially white writers, adopt, a kind of nostalgia for a time when stakes were higher and everybody was listened to, and everyone was in the café. There's something dead about that to me. But that's not the same as saying let's abandon modernism. There's something very urgent about the utopian currents of modernism in particular right now. It feels like the culture is kind of trying to close those currents down because they are subversive, and are still potentially disruptive and dangerous.

RACHEL KUSHNER

I wanted to talk about people who take up one another's work even across time. I wasn't that interested in Fitzgerald and Malcolm Lowry until I read Deleuze's essay about those two writers. I like thinking about the ways in which writers traverse the cultural imaginary into other realms.

HARI KUNZRU

There's a particular sort of British position with regards to that. There's a generation who grew up in the particularly gray, austerity, postwar world, and they were looking at cars with fins and movie stars. They saw America as a magical world of consumer promise. I am thinking about people like Martin Amis, who are absolutely enslaved to a notion of America as bigger and more colorful. Now, with the globalization of pop culture, that doesn't function in the same way. But in the eighties and nineties in London there was a publication whose motto was high culture for lowbrows, or low culture for highbrows, something like that. They would write long essays about Baudrillard and Schwarzenegger. It was a very cool thing to do, at that particular moment. Irony took over and no one was allowed to be serious about anything. But now look at the mess we're in.

RIVKA GALCHEN

I feel like it's a writer instinct or just a thinker instinct to be out of place. You want to displace yourself, maybe in time or geography, or whatever it is. You think, "When I'm comfortable and I know what's going on, I'm pretty stupid." And then, "When I'm uncomfortable and I'm aware that I'm not really keyed in and I'm not the expert, I'm in a better position." It's that instinct to mess it up a little less, by being dislocated in some way.

RACHEL KUSHNER

I totally agree. Part of being a writer is looking for this way in which you are entering some new realm, or you have to navigate it in some way. I've never really written any pop culture into fiction, but I want to now. There's a lot to be done with pop culture. I wanted to write a novel about a female version of Riff Raff. And then James Franco played him in the movie *Spring Breakers.* When I saw it I felt like it had a transcendent and amazing, lyrical, almost biblical treatment of what's considered to be very low American pop culture. It really blew my mind. I saw more possibility for myself with using hot bodies in Florida. Just kidding.

4

Edward Albee & Paul Auster

WITH JEANNETTE SEAVER

JEANNETTE SEAVER

What brings us three together tonight is Samuel Beckett, his legacy, his influence on literature. Also, as far as I'm concerned, what brings me here is my lifelong friendship with Mr. Beckett. I came to know him through my late husband, Dick Seaver, who was directly responsible for bringing the work of Beckett in English to America, and he was Mr. Albee's editor, too.

When Dick was in Paris, working on James Joyce, he discovered this unknown Irish author, who was writing in French. He couldn't quite get that. He bought all the books, read them in French, and dropped a note to the French publisher asking to meet the mysterious man. Dick wanted to publish some of his work in a literary review called *Merlin*, which at the time he was running with two or three other poets and writers in Paris. He'd heard that Beckett had a novel called *Watt* that had never been published in English. In fact this work had been systematically rejected by the entire English publishing industry. Beckett was discouraged and had put the manuscript in a drawer. He'd decided never to pull it out. But Dick pursued him, and insisted.

In his memoir Dick writes about how he took his bike across Paris with a letter to Mr. Beckett (whom he did not know at the time), soliciting the manuscript of the novel. He didn't hear back for weeks, but then one rainy night Mr. Beckett showed up at the door. He pulled out the manuscript from his raincoat, handed it to Dick, and asked him to let him know what he thought of it. And then he left.

Dick and the rest of the other writers and poets of *Merlin* spent that entire night taking turns at reading *Watt* out loud. The next morning they decided they had to publish it as a book. They were not established as a publishing house, since they only had the journal. But they decided that they would look for money to do it. They made an offer, and Beckett was thrilled and surprised. He used to call Dick and his group "the *Merlin* juveniles," because they were goofy and *sympathique*. Dick was so passionate with the discovery of Beckett's writing! It was really a literary explosion for him.

He'd written an essay in *Merlin* about Beckett, and that essay made its way to America. In New York, a new publisher at a new publishing house called Grove Press read the piece. He decided to fly to Paris to meet Dick, and hopefully also that unknown Irish writer. The rest is history. Grove Press became Beckett's publisher, and Dick became the editor-in-chief of Grove Press and became Beckett's editor, this side of the Atlantic.

Later on Beckett also asked Dick to translate three wonderful short stories: "The Calmative," "The End," and "The Expelled." They were all published in *Merlin*. After that,

Beckett asked Dick if he could translate *Godot*. At that point Dick was finishing his edition of Joyce and he declined, which of course was something he regretted the rest of his life. However, the world was well served having Beckett do his own writing and translating, although he hated translating his own work.

Some time ago, Mr. Albee said in a *Paris Review* interview that Beckett was the one playwright that he unabashedly admired. I'd like to ask him about this.

EDWARD ALBEE

Yes, well, I'm a very selfish person, and I admire most the things that I get most from.

JEANNETTE SEAVER

At what point did Beckett enter your life?

EDWARD ALBEE

Nothing can come from osmosis, unless you participate in it. To a certain extent, I was aware the first time I read a sentence by Beckett, and the first time I saw or heard words by Beckett, that I was in the presence of somebody and something—not only a person but a *thing*—who was absolutely extraordinary and amazing. Every once in a while, you get to say that word, *Wow!* That's what I felt of my first experience with Beckett: *Wow!*

PAUL AUSTER

In my case it's a bit different, because I'm two decades younger than Edward. When I first encountered Beckett, I was nineteen or so, so we're talking about the mid-sixties.

At that point he was already a world-famous writer. Interestingly, I didn't start with his plays but with his prose. At first I resisted it—and this is something that has happened to me with several of the writers who later became my favorites. I was reading *Malone Dies* and I didn't quite get into the swing of it. So I put it down and went back to it a few months later. It was then that I understood that the prose was of such a high level that it was stupefying. The great writers, the truly original ones, produce work so different from what anyone else does that you don't even know what to make of it at first. That's why it takes a while to absorb what they're doing. Emily Dickinson is also like this—so brilliant, and so idiosyncratic. You need a little time to get into this kind of work.

JEANNETTE SEAVER

You know, the philosopher Jacques Derrida said that Beckett's work makes the limits of our language tremble.

EDWARD ALBEE

Pretty good!

PAUL AUSTER

In 2006, on the event of Beckett's one-hundredth birthday, I was the editor of a new collection of all his work with Grove Press, called *The Grove Centenary Edition*. It's pretty close to a complete Beckett in four volumes. I cleaned up all the typos, if I did nothing else, and asked four writers to contribute prefaces. Volume Three had all his plays, and I could think of no one better to write this part about Beckett than Edward.

EDWARD ALBEE

I wish I could say I am as fond of his poetry as I am of the rest of his work, but that's my fault, perhaps his, I don't know . . . *Beckett's* fault.

PAUL AUSTER

Beckett's journey as a novelist and a prose writer, a fiction writer, is different from his journey as a playwright because he started out writing fiction when he was very young. I don't think he wrote his first play until he was in his forties. His early prose is heavily influenced by Joyce. It's ornate. They were of course fellow Irishmen, and they were friends, and Beckett was an admiring younger writer who had become deeply involved with Joyce—and this may explain his decision to write in French later, after World War II. In order to unbury himself out from under the familiar.

I think he was in his late twenties when his book of stories, *More Pricks Than Kicks*, was published. There are some terrific things in it, but it's not up to what he would do later. We already talked about *Watt*, but I think it's important to mention how this book came into being. Beckett was living in France. It was World War II. He was part of an underground resistance group in Paris. His job was, I think, to carry messages from one person to another—as he dismissively put it years later, "boy-scout stuff," but it wasn't, because it was actually very dangerous. When the cell was broken, and his best friend was arrested and later killed by the Nazis, Beckett and his wife, or the woman who would become his wife, had to leave Paris. They eventually made their way down to the free zone, in the south, in the town of Roussillon. There, Beckett found work as an agricultural laborer, he picked potatoes for two years. They had no money, and it was the desperation of wartime in France.

There is an anecdote I particularly like about this period of Beckett's life. It came to me from Wally Shawn, the playwright and actor. He told me that when he was acting in the film *The Princess Bride*—which maybe some of you have seen, the terrific children's movie—he found out that the big French actor in the movie, André the Giant, the professional wrestler, had been a little boy growing up in Roussillon during the war. Beckett befriended André the Giant before he became a giant and drove him to school in the truck every morning.

Anyway, Beckett said that he wrote *Watt* as an exercise to keep his sanity. I think he mostly wrote it at night. It's a crazy book. It doesn't resemble any other novel I've read. And I also think it's one of the funniest books in the English language.

EDWARD ALBEE

What an amazing composer Beckett was! Just listening to his prose, it stops being prose, and it becomes music, it doesn't become poetry. It still retains its sense.

PAUL AUSTER

Each great writer has his own music, but Beckett's has a particular purity to it that burns through.

EDWARD ALBEE

It doesn't hurt being Irish, of course.

PAUL AUSTER

Perhaps not, but there are a lot of lousy Irish writers, too.

JEANNETTE SEAVER

Music was very important to Beckett. He played the piano. And the only instrument that he brought to his little house in Ussy was an upright piano. Up-straight, upright. He built that house, and then he was in the living room and he saw people looking at *him*, and he started crawling around, until he got a gardener or architect to build a wall.

PAUL AUSTER

I wanted to tell you about my first meeting with Beckett. I lived in France in the early seventies, and I became good friends with Joan Mitchell, the American painter. Joan had been married to Barney Rosset, the publisher of Grove Press, and was a very good friend of Beckett's. One day we were talking about his work, and she asked me if I would like to meet him. "Of course I would like to meet him," I said. And she said, "Well, just write him a letter and say I said so." I did as she told me and wrote to him saying Joan Mitchell said . . . and he wrote back two or three days later and suggested we meet at la Closerie des Lilas to have a drink together.

I went, but I was trembling in my boots. I don't think I've ever been more nervous about meeting a human being in my life. To me, he was the God of Literature, and even if I had been going to meet Winston Churchill, I wouldn't have been half as intimidated. But he turned out to be very nice, direct, gentle, funny, engaging, and at one point he mentioned that he had just finished an English translation of the first novel he had written in French, *Mercier and Camier.* He had won the Nobel Prize a couple years before, and his French publisher wanted to get as much of his work published as possible. So, after writing the book in 1946, Beckett finally allowed it to be published in 1970, and now he was doing the English version. And he said to me, "You know, it's really not a very good book, and I've cut out about twenty-five percent of the original in the English translation." And I said, "Why?" (I had read it in French.) "Why would you do that? It's such a great book." And he said, "No, really, not very good, it's not very good at all." I was so young at the time, so optimistic about life, I jumped in and said, "No, no, it's really a wonderful book. I disagree with you." And then we went on to talk about other things. About ten minutes later, apropos of nothing, he interrupted me and said, "You really liked it, huh? You really think it's good?" And I said, "Yeah, I really think it's good." This was a great revelation to me. No artist can ever understand the value of his own work. It's amazing to think about it. But there he was, the greatest writer living in the world at the time, and he had not a clue about how good his book was.

JEANNETTE SEAVER

We had seen *Godot* when it was first produced in Paris, at the Théâtre de Babylone. Dick and I were dating at that point and we went to see it, and there were fourteen people in the theater at that point, and very mixed reviews. Well, ten years later, he'd had the Nobel, and the same production with the same cast was put on at the Théâtre National de l'Odéon, you know, big-time, very formal gala opening, and Beckett refused to go. We went and it was a standing ovation. The same reviewers who had put him down ten years before were now singing his praise.

So we arrived at the Dôme, where Beckett was waiting, and his head was in his hands, and he was in total depression, and I said, "Sam, this was a wonderful, wonderful production. It was great." And he says, "You don't know what you're talking about. It's a terrible play. It's rubbish." So it continued. He never thought it was a good play. He was really in deep depression most of his life about his work.

PAUL AUSTER

I don't know if anyone has been reading Beckett's letters. I've gone through the first two volumes, and it's incredible to read how, just as he's beginning to acquire some traction in the literary world and become read and even well known, he's writing to his friends and basically saying they can't imagine how deeply he despises his own work.

Edward, I just want to know, when did you first encounter Beckett—the work and the man?

EDWARD ALBEE

I met Beckett and encountered Beckett at exactly the moment I read my first sentence by Beckett. I don't think you need to meet people in person to know them, or to meet them. I don't think that's necessary.

JEANNETTE SEAVER

Was that before *The Zoo Story*?

EDWARD ALBEE

Of course. Everything was before *The Zoo Story*! I know that I met Beckett the first time I experienced his work.

PAUL AUSTER

Was it a play, was it a work of fiction?

EDWARD ALBEE

Plays are also works of fiction.

PAUL AUSTER

We're going to go around and around tonight, I can see that. We're sounding more and more like two characters from *Watt*.

JEANNETTE SEAVER

I was told that there was a bus driver in Roussillon whose name was Godot, and indeed there was always a cluster of people waiting for the damn bus that never seemed to arrive—*En attendant Godot.*

PAUL AUSTER

It seems as plausible an explanation as any other.

JEANNETTE SEAVER

Paul, I'd like to ask you, when you started writing, you were very under the influence of Beckett, perhaps?

PAUL AUSTER

Yes. I was very young. I couldn't really see my way around him. As Edward says in his introduction to the third volume of *The Centenary Edition*, he puts up a blockage; it's hard to see a way around him. I couldn't, and therefore I really stuck to just writing poetry. I thought there was no way I could contribute anything to the novel, even though that's what I was dying to do. It took me a while to . . . what? To grow up? To feel a certain indifference.

It gets to a point where you say, "Well, Beckett, you

know, that's enough. I don't need you anymore. I'm throwing you off my back, I love your work, but I have to do my own stuff." Then it became possible for me to write.

EDWARD ALBEE

Because it would be easier than trying to do something that good?

PAUL AUSTER

You always want to do the best you can, but as you say, very beautifully in your little piece, you can't imitate. I mean, imitation is just a ridiculous exercise in stupidity.

JEANNETTE SEAVER

But Pinter's early play *The Caretaker* was very, very much under the influence of Beckett.

EDWARD ALBEE

Not a bad choice.

JEANNETTE SEAVER

He then grew into his own voice.

EDWARD ALBEE

This also happened to Beckett himself, after his first few plays. If you listen to Beckett, you get so much more out of it than simply reading it.

PAUL AUSTER

Yes, but later on, there were some late works, *Company*, for example. I thought it was one of the best things he'd ever written. And he was, I guess, deep into his seventies at the time, and he found some less rigid way of expressing himself then. The plays just got better and better all the way through.

Questions from the Audience

In the later editions of Martin Esslin's work The Theatre of the Absurd, *he identifies you as a protégé of this movement that encompasses Beckett, but Ionesco and Adamov and Genet, as well. And I was wondering—*

EDWARD ALBEE

You mean *The Theatre of the Absurd*, that preposterous bit of misinformation.

Yes. It's since been kind of torn apart, but I was wondering, to what extent do you agree with that assessment of you as a protégé or inheritor of this tradition of the absurd?

EDWARD ALBEE

I don't really understand most of these terms that critics use to define things. I can only judge by what I respond to and believe. I don't think much about the concept of the Theatre of the Absurd. The simplification of that is, the definition of something that makes absolutely no sense, and we have to believe the fact that something makes absolutely no sense . . . This puzzles me. I don't know much of what most people think that they're talking about when they talk about literature.

You spoke earlier of Beckett and Pinter finding their own voice. This actually applies to both of you. When did each of you find your own personal voice after getting around Beckett's "blockage"?

EDWARD ALBEE

I think one of the things that allowed me to find the individuality of my voice was being able to hear it, to listen to it, to respond to it, to what it was saying, and the way it was saying it. When I was kid, I thought I was going to be a composer. I have absolutely no talent as a composer. My concept of a string quartet wouldn't pass muster anywhere, though I loved classical music and I still do, probably more than any other art form, painting and sculpture being a close second, even more than literature. I find that all of the arts relate to each other profoundly. Composers are writers, and writers are composers, and sculptors are this or that. It's all the same thing. It is a different manifestation of the same thing.

PAUL AUSTER

I agree, I don't understand the labels that critics and journalists give. You're the absurd theater man; I'm the postmodernist novelist. I have no idea what postmodernism is.

EDWARD ALBEE

I'm glad you don't know.

PAUL AUSTER

Jeannette quoted Jacques Derrida before, a writer I've never read, because I found him impossible to understand. And yet, again and again, students have written whole papers, even books, about Derrida's influence on my writing. So I am as befuddled as Edward. As he said, you just listen to that voice, and if you can hear it, it starts to sing inside you.

What I'm trying to say is that if it's working, it's working, and you know when it's working, and you know when it's not. In my own case, since I was such a literary boy, I was carrying literature on my back for years. I hit a kind of crisis when I was in my late twenties, maybe thirty, and I stopped writing for a year. I didn't do anything, and then when I was ready to write again, I didn't care anymore. Those books were not on my back. And it's been going that way now for decades.

EDWARD ALBEE

We never hear our own voices. We hear the voices that we have invented.

PAUL AUSTER

Okay. That's a more precise way of putting it. Whatever it is that's in your head, you hear it. And I don't know where it comes from. It probably comes from many different places all at once. It's music, yes. Everything I've ever written, all the novels I've written begin with a buzz in my head, a rhythm that comes before the words, and I try to follow that music as I'm writing the book.

Do all three of you agree that you prefer the prose and plays to the poetry of Beckett, and, if so, what is present in the plays and the prose that is absent in the poetry?

EDWARD ALBEE

I'm not even sure that Beckett thought in those terms. Did he think of himself as a novelist or a playwright? But hell, he didn't need to have done the poetry, too. It's not *bad*. It's pretty good poetry. But his accomplishments in letting us understand the nature of the communication of the arts is so much higher in the prose and in the drama.

PAUL AUSTER

I agree, but I have a soft spot for the poetry. There are two or three beautiful poems and some very good lines in the others. He only wrote about thirty poems. Maybe if he'd done more, it would have become extraordinary, but I think his gifts lay elsewhere, and he went to those other places.

What are your own individual interpretations of Waiting for Godot*?*

EDWARD ALBEE

With any luck, it's the same as Beckett's. Why would you be interested in any of our interpretations?

To be honest with you, I can't understand it.

EDWARD ALBEE

It's all there.

JEANNETTE SEAVER

You can't understand *Godot*? Oh, my god. Oh, my god. When Dick was dating me, in his passion for Beckett, he took me to the Théâtre de Babylone, and I was a kid, and I suppose he told me later it was a test: had I failed, I would not have married him, or he would not have married me, rather. And, I got it. There's nothing not to get! I've gotta talk to you. It is so simple.

You can have any kind of private interpretation. It fits. It's okay. It's very, very human, very funny. It's *hilarious.* Sense of humor is something we didn't talk about. He has an enormous sense of humor.

It sounds like he himself didn't understand it, either.

EDWARD ALBEE

We all lie when we say we don't understand what we're doing. The difference is we don't always want to take responsibility for it.

I would like to ask about the creative process that you were speaking about, that you have to listen to your own voice, and if you think that after having a crisis you can again hear that voice.

EDWARD ALBEE

No. Writer's block is gibberish.

PAUL AUSTER

Well, you have to live through certain tough patches, and I did. Then I started writing again . . . I don't know, it felt inevitable. The overall impulse to do it, I didn't question anymore. But you can't listen to us for advice. When young people come to me and say they want to be writers, I say, "Don't do it."

EDWARD ALBEE

Don't *be* it, *do* it.

PAUL AUSTER

I say that because what you're getting into is a life of loneliness, poverty, and neglect. That's all you're asking for.

EDWARD ALBEE

And if you're bad enough, you'll make a lot of money.

PAUL AUSTER

If someone listens to my advice, then that person wasn't meant to be a writer.

5

Téa Obreht & Charles Simic

CHARLES SIMIC

I have purchased many books over the years here, some very nice rare books, and I've also sold more books than I've bought. Today, as I was walking up Broadway, I remembered selling one particular book. This was roughly in 1960, I lived on East Thirteenth Street, just off University Place. I worked at NYU in the payroll department, and I used to get paid on Friday. I would be broke by Monday, but I don't really remember how. It was Saturday morning and I was totally, completely broke, and there was rent to pay and other things to be paid, and I had sold all my books worth selling, but I had one left that a guy who was living at the apartment where I lived, that little place, gave me. It was the *Oxford Latin Dictionary*, and I just felt that this was an incredibly impressive book of probably five thousand pages that I had to have, though I never consulted it. In my desperation, I decided to sell it. As I said, it was Saturday morning, and the street was empty, though in this part of New York in those days, all of New York, really, on Saturday morning the streets were empty. The Strand was open, it was nine o'clock or later. I carried this really heavy book, which was so huge, the kind of thing that you need lecterns in libraries to sit on. I brought the book to the front where you sold books, and it was this sourpuss who never broke a smile, but just gave you the price of the books. I thought ten bucks for sure, maybe fifteen, which was a lot of money in those days. He offered me five. I was stunned, but decided to sell it anyway to avoid carrying the damn thing back about five or six blocks. That was just one of the many times and memorable moments at the Strand Book Store.

I came to New York from Chicago, in 1958, by myself. I was twenty years old, and kind of lonely. I lived in furnished rooms and fleabag hotels in the Village. I didn't want to go back to Chicago, because when I left, my friends had asked me what was I going to do in New York if I did not know anybody here. I dismissed their words because I had always wanted to come back to New York, a city where I'd first lived after I came from Europe. Not enough jazz, not enough tears, or not enough galleries, or not enough, on and on, and you know. I was a snob. So I came to New York, and I didn't know anyone. I lived in truly dumps—hotels where you knew that the room that you occupied, there were murders committed, that there was major violence. The carpet hadn't been changed in thirty years. And in those days, people really chain-smoked. I wrote a poem about one of these dumps, "Self-Portrait in Bed." It's fun to write about these things viewed from a distance, when you are in your seventies. You realize you were an asshole, but you look at it with great affection: "How did this guy survive, on the grossest street?"

I also have several poems about libraries. I've spent a lot of time in libraries, and the great thing about such places, or a great bookstore like this, is that you walk around and suddenly you see something, and find yourself gasping and saying, "I can't believe this book exists." You sort of leap and grab it. You think somebody's going to beat you to it. Those are very exciting moments. I wrote a poem about this dedicated to the late Mexican poet Octavio Paz, because one day we were talking about books that had fantastic titles that turned out to be mediocre.

One nice thing about a lot of poems is that you have no memory how they were written. Sometimes it takes months, sometimes even years. With the titles you often say to yourself that something sounds good and that you'll work around it. About three years ago, I wrote "1938," but it had occurred to me before. One day I was reading something—I don't know what exactly, something about history—and 1938 was mentioned. I thought, that was the year I was born, and a lot of things were going on. I found it amazing that I was a little kid in a crib trying to pull a pillow off my booties, and all these things were happening in the world. So it occurred to me that I wanted to find out what was going on, simultaneously with my early days, and in years before I would have gone to the library and gotten some almanacs and looked up things, and so forth. I Googled 1938. And in less than a minute, I found pretty much everything that happened. I was interested in more or less historical things, events in popular culture, so on and so forth. I got an immense amount of information, and made a mistake: I printed it. It turned out to be eighty pages of stuff. Then I had to pick and choose, because there was so much going on at the same time, it took a long time. I think the poem was finally finished about three years ago, but it took maybe a couple of years, if not more. I kept putting things in and pulling things out. I knew it couldn't be a very long poem because it'd go on and on. There were so many tempting options. It's the only poem I've written like that.

I also very clearly remember how "My Turn to Confess" occurred to me. We were talking about interviews, and somebody asked what I thought about confessional poetry. I said that, if the poet is a good liar, that's fine, as long as he or she doesn't tell the truth. Afterwards I felt guilty, you know, what sort of wise guy said that.

TÉA OBREHT

I'll start off confessing that I've been a fan of Mr. Simic's poetry. I'm a fellow Yugoslav, and more importantly, I feel, a fellow Belgrader. So I want to start off by asking you about your childhood memories of that city.

CHARLES SIMIC

Like with any war child, I had plenty of memories. I've mentioned this many times, but I was born in 1938, and on April 6, 1941, Belgrade was bombed by the Nazis. We lived right in the heart of the city, and I think it was probably one morning when a bomb hit the building across the street, and pretty much destroyed it. I was in bed, I was two years old, and I flew out of bed, and landed on the floor, and what I vaguely remember: sort of bright lights, and the building was on fire, and broken glass, and my mother was in the next room, and picking me off of the floor. She carried me away, we went into the cellar, as we used to do. I grew up in an occupied country that was occupied mostly by Germans, but there were some parts that were occupied by Italians, or by Hungarians. There was also a civil war going on. Yugoslavia, depending how you count, began maybe three, four, five, maybe six factions, killing each other in the countryside. Actually, being in the city was much safer than being in some small village. You know how it is if you live and write in the heart of a city. Streets used to be full of kids in those days, and we used to play screaming, and those years they could stop you from going down and playing with those kids, and my memories even from second year are vivid. Then in 1944, the city got bombed by the Allies. We were pro-Allies, so they were going to hit the Germans, but they never hit them but us instead. There was plenty of action, and my memories are extremely vivid. The end of the war is something I've written about. There were dead bodies on the street, people are hanged from telephone poles, there were millions of things going on. Then after the war, in 1953, it was communism and so forth, the restive depression. We were starving after the war. There was nothing to eat, that's what I remember of those years.

On the other hand, I don't have many bad memories. There was really some awful stuff, but I had a great time growing up. I sometimes think that this is something about me that is a little defective in some way, like some brick fell on my head, because I really had a ball. I was always playing on the street. Parents were all busy, my father was in Italy at the end of the war and didn't come back, and my mother . . . we were running loose like all the other kids. Paradise. Years later, I've met people who grew up in war-zone Berlin and a wonderful woman my age who grew up in Warsaw in 1944, which was awful. But she said, "Charlie, you're forgetting one thing: we were so happy, because there was no school." She was absolutely right, I'd forgotten.

TÉA OBREHT

Since there was no school, what was your relationship to literature growing up at that time?

CHARLES SIMIC

Once you could read, you read anything you could get your hands on. Winter came, and crummy weather. Before the war, before comics came, in Yugoslavia, all the American comic books were translated, all kinds of trashy literature, and then after that, just out of sheer boredom, my father had a big library, and we read a lot of books, and enjoyed some of them. In school, we read Yugoslav literature, we had to read poetry, but I don't remember in school being interested in what we read. Like everywhere else in the world, literature taught in school, especially poetry, was a form of punishment. Before I came to the U.S., I was in a school in Paris for a year, and it was the same thing. We read great nineteenth century French poets—Baudelaire, Rimbaud, Verlaine—and we had to memorize the poems. Teachers were just lazy old civil servants, who had the class take turns reciting these poems. It was something terrible for me, because I spoke French with a heavy accent, and my fellow students really enjoyed it. So the literature that made an impression on me was my private reading in idle hours. I read things that are ridiculous for a very young reader, things by Dickens, or Balzac, things that really aren't books. Besides reading, there was no other way to spend a rainy day.

TÉA OBREHT

You've been a city-dweller for much of your life: first Belgrade, then Paris, Chicago, and New York. It's no surprise that cityscapes figure really prominently in your work. What moves you about cities?

CHARLES SIMIC

My imagination is activated by cities in a way it isn't in the country. I've been living in the countryside since 1973, in a little village. I feel at home there and I love it, but I don't notice ten percent of what I see in a city. There, the moment I'm on the street, and I look down the block, and see people coming this way and that way, I look at faces, right away, you associate things . . . My imagination is stimulated, entertained. When I travel I feel instantly at home in cities. I know how to talk to city people, and even if I love being in the country, it's not the same.

TÉA OBREHT

Would you say that there's something universal about cities that transcends geographical locations?

CHARLES SIMIC

Oh, yes, I think so. There was a lot I loved about Belgrade before I went to Paris. In those days there were plenty of movie houses, and we were close, so we'd skip school, and stand there for hours looking at photographs of Randolph Scott with his pistol. A lot of stuff meant absolutely nothing to me. I loved the modern part of the city, where you felt like you were in the twentieth century. The thing about Eastern Europe, especially in those days, was that by the time you got to the outskirts of a city, you were in the nineteenth century, and this is true not just of Belgrade, but some people say it happens also in Sofia, or Bucharest. If you went thirty miles farther, you were in the eighteenth century. If you kept going, you ended up in the tenth century.

When I got to Paris, again, I really liked the modern part of the city. I found some pretty beautiful old quarters, the Champs-Élysées, the movie theaters, the gardens and nightclubs, and I thought it was like Belgrade, but fifty times bigger. Of course, when I arrived to New York I felt this could not be beaten.

TÉA OBREHT

I grew up in places that had a really rich heritage, but I never appreciated it until after I left. Then people would ask me, and I realized it was *beautiful*, but I never paid attention to the old part at all. Now, you're a self-professed insomniac. Much of your poetry has to do with nighttime loneliness and spectatorship of strange moments, and surreal entities as a result of solitude in the dark. I'm finding myself very lucky right now to be writing on a daily basis. But while I wrote *The Tiger's Wife*, most of those writing hours were between midnight and five in the morning. Do you consider insomnia a part of your writing routine?

CHARLES SIMIC

It was, and I think there was also a practical aspect about this. When I lived in New York, I worked during the day; I had office jobs, nine-to-five. When I left the office I would go out to bars, maybe at five o'clock, and have a beer. If I got home by midnight, that was an early night. I had infinite energy in those days, so I always sat up late and wrote. I used to smoke, and sitting up late at night, I'd smoke, listening to records, and whatever. Now I don't smoke anymore, plus my eyes aren't as great, so I don't do it. Most of my writing these days is done fairly early in the morning. Also at dinner hour I always get inspired.

With poetry, nobody can write for eight hours. I also write a lot of prose and books about this and that, and you really work, six or seven hours, you can spend day after day on an essay. That's not the case with poetry. Fiction writers really have to *work*. Poets, I mean, very, very rarely you'll have a kind of binge. Most of the time, things come to you. "In Confession" was probably jotted down in a restaurant while I was waiting for a dinner. With poetry, later on you tinker with it, you revise it endlessly, but it's not something you say, "Oh! I have to finish this poem! I have to do it *today*!" A ten-line poem? No, that's not how you start. You can't say to yourself, you'll write a five-line poem. So, how do you do that? You endlessly tinker something that's much longer, like a sort of an accordion thing—it gets longer, shorter, longer, shorter, longer, shorter. Months go by, and one day you look at it, and you see that there are only five lines that are worth keeping. It's a very different way of working than the way a fiction writer works.

TÉA OBREHT

Worth trying, though, I think, even for fiction. The problem that I have is that anything I write is way too long, and so it's usually only the five lines . . .

CHARLES SIMIC

It's always easier to be a poet. I like paring down. It's astonishing when you realize you spent months, sometimes even years, deluding yourself. Once I had this sort of sequence of poems, something about New York City, I don't even remember what it was—but it was four or five pages, and then one day I'd reduced it to a dozen lines, and it seemed fine. But there's no way to generalize about poets. Everybody writes differently.

TÉA OBREHT

Have you ever been surprised to learn something about yourself, your preoccupations, your thoughts, after looking back on completed work?

CHARLES SIMIC

That's the interesting thing about writing. And it comes slowly. We don't reread poems, or think about it. One doesn't look at your poems from a distance, or critically, the way you look at somebody else's. You have other things to do. So they come as a surprise. The first time I published a poem was in 1959, such a long time ago. After forty years or more, it just hit me how much violence there is in my early poems. I'm a person who really dislikes violence. I do not associate myself with it, but there are so many hangings, and so many atrocities in those verses. Really they are not just only biographical elements, every time that I've seen something like that happening in the world . . . The extent of it kind of surprised me. Somebody once asked me directly if I was obsessed with violence. We lack the self-knowledge to admit this and I'm good-natured.

TÉA OBREHT

This leads to my next and final question. It's something that I've been asked myself, and due to your background, I'm sure you frequently come across this kind of query. Do you feel that your commitment to poetry, or indeed to any art form, comes with a sense of social or political obligation?

CHARLES SIMIC

No, I don't. If you look at American poetry, you find Walt Whitman, who was certainly aware of the Civil War. He wrote poems and prose. But Emily Dickinson does not mention it directly. She lived in her house in Amherst, and her room looked at this church across the street, where there were weekly funerals of young boys she knew who had died in the Civil War. You would expect her to pen something on that life, and though she wrote beautiful letters of condolence, she didn't write a poem about it. I've never thought this made her a lesser poet. It isn't an obligation. I've written about politics because I'm always interested in it, and I read newspapers. But I think what I dislike about that sort of pressure is that it implies that writers have this special vision and a certain obligation to say something about current affairs, because they have sensitive souls and certain qualities that the rest of the world is waiting to hear. I think back on the poetry readings held against the war. I participated and I went to them, and everybody who worked on them had their heart in the right place, but the poetry really sucked. Nothing of that time remained, and for an excellent reason, which was that it was worthless. They were not even as good as editorials against the war. That kind of cured me. Also, we both come from Yugoslavia, where communism was in everyone's school literature. In those days it was like Stalinism, telling us about the happy workers who are digging ditches and working in mines.

I hate that stuff, but if you look at my poems, in every book there are at least four or five poems that deal with that reality which we describe as politics.

TÉA OBREHT

But it's liberating to hear that you feel you can do it as a personal reaction to something as opposed to some sort of required response.

CHARLES SIMIC

I mean the idea of ordering somebody to do something escapes me.

Questions from the Audience

What do you find more challenging, writing poetry or working on translations?

CHARLES SIMIC

Everything is hard. Writing essays is hard. Translations have special difficulties. This is a vast subject, but I'll narrow it down to this: I have poems that were written a long time ago, and I know that perhaps, in most cases, they're not all that they could have been, but I've never touched them again. Because it's mine and, you know, forget it. On the other hand, translation is an endless thing. Reading is awful because of translation. You sometimes work for years translating poems. Once it's done I don't look at it anymore, but then once the book has been around for thirty years, one of those translations may come up, and then, instantly, you start looking at the translation and see how this could be improved, I see some turn of phrase that just escaped me at the time. Translations seem never finished, and if I had time, I might end up retranslating some of my favorite poets. Vasko Popa was a very difficult poet to translate, because his poems are short, and when I look at them I see the problem. They're awkward. It's not that you missed the meaning, but that it sounds like a translation, and the solution that eluded you all these years is already there. This happens with translations. When you're doing your own poetry, you can simply say, "Bye-bye. I don't even want to look at this thing again."

I have a question for Ms. Obreht. I read The Tiger's Wife *and there are many layers in the story, there are subplots in the subplots, like that part about the hunter, or the butcher who wants to be a musician. All these stories render depth to the main story. How does that work? When you start off you have one layer?*

TÉA OBREHT

It was my first time writing, so every aspect of writing the novel was a complete learning experience, and half the time I was not sure, I was just trying. Eventually, what kept me going on to deeper layers was the feeling that it was too superficial, or that I didn't understand properly what a certain character was doing or where it came from. So I would write something that would serve as an explanation. I know for some people it worked and for some people it didn't, but the effect this had for me was that it created a 3-D picture. The layers expanded in directions that I couldn't really account for and hadn't planned on, and so eventually I ended up having to storyboard it, which was the practical solution. It was the first time a project had taken off and left me behind.

I'd like Mr. Simic to talk about some of the poets he has admired over the years.

CHARLES SIMIC

Whitman, and Dickinson, who I think is my favorite poet. Wallace Stevens and Dickinson are two poets that I can read every day of my life. There are others, lots of poets that I adore. I mentioned those French poets that I hated at the time when I had to recite their verses and humiliate myself, but I realized many, many years later that saying those poems aloud, even in French, had a huge influence on me. Baudelaire is still one of my favorite poets. I started writing without realizing I was trying to imitate something that I had heard.

In your writing process, how do you rank image, sound, history, and memory?

CHARLES SIMIC

It depends; I've written poems starting from every one of those things. Sometimes you just have a sound. You go around mumbling, and somebody asks, "What are you mumbling about?" And then you realize you are doing it. When I think I have a great idea, it never works. You can spend months working on it and then you realize that it was not a good idea. With images, something suddenly pops out of your memory. Like in my poem "Paradise," where I did see a couple. This was somewhere around Ninth Avenue, maybe on Forty-ninth Street. I had been at a poker game, though I wasn't a gambler, I didn't have any money. When I left, I walked back to my house here in the Village, it was a nice morning, dawn. And I did meet those two. I didn't think about them for years. The book came out 1990 more or less, and the poem was probably written in the 1980s. And everything else came back, all those memories. I find even more interesting are those poems that start with a phrase or an image that you have no idea where it comes from. But you want it so much that your task is to sort of invent a poem to go around it. It's great. It's an adventure, where you have no idea where you're going. It may not work, but it's a lot of fun.

6

Alison Bechdel & Katie Roiphe

KATIE ROIPHE

Alison is one of the most exciting, innovative, and interesting writers today. I'm thrilled to be here, as many people will have suspected from my near-fawning *New York Times* review of *Are You My Mother?* The editors were like, "This is too much." So, aside from that somewhat undignified review, it seems that people love this book in an unusual way, and I want to delve into that, the why's and the how's of that.

ALISON BECHDEL

I just today read this very interesting review of the book by Heather Love. Do you know her? She's an academic. She thinks the book itself is a transitional object. In *Are You My Mother?* I write about Donald Winnicott's idea of how teddy bears or blankets function as transitional objects for kids, and Love made this funny case that the book itself was a transitional object for me, I guess.

KATIE ROIPHE

Perhaps she meant for readers as well. It's interesting that they should have such a strong identification with this book. The story you're telling is so quirky, so idiosyncratic, so specific, so unique to you—and yet even people who didn't have that kind of mother, but still had some other kind of difficult mother, somehow really "identify," though this word is too simple to describe for how they feel about it. Do you think your book has helped them to look at their experience in a different way?

ALISON BECHDEL

I feel sort of like a therapist lately. I'm getting all these really intense emails from people. I had that same experience after writing *Fun Home*—people would come up to me and say, "Oh, this is just like my family." Then they would proceed to describe a family nothing like mine. I came to think that it was just the act of telling the truth about a family, or revealing family secrets, that people found empowering or exciting. I knew that my story in *Fun Home* was highly personal and idiosyncratic. Since people seemed to relate anyhow, I got emboldened to push it even further in this book about my mother. I think it is a very deeply strange book.

KATIE ROIPHE

A lot of people tell the truth about their families in memoirs, in novels. I think it must be something about the *way* you tell the truth about your family.

ALISON BECHDEL

You don't think it's just because I have archival backup, like diary entries and newspaper clippings?

KATIE ROIPHE

That is quite interesting, but maybe it's partly that you're writing in your own reluctance. You write the whole process you go through. You're writing into it the difficulty, which I don't think is very common, and the kind of guilt, and the whole tormented compulsion.

ALISON BECHDEL

I tried to do that and I wonder if in this book about my mother, which ultimately became about writing the book, if that wasn't maybe a little too much.

KATIE ROIPHE

You have this great quote from Virginia Woolf. After she wrote *To the Lighthouse*, she says, "I ceased to be obsessed by my mother. I no longer hear her voice; I do not see her. I expressed some very long-felt and deeply felt emotion, and in expressing it, I explained it, and then laid it to rest." Did you, too, feel this way after writing this book, like you resolved it?

ALISON BECHDEL

Not at all. I'd hoped that I'd make that happen. Yet, what I learned with my book *Fun Home* is that books aren't really over when they're over. They keep living in the world, and people's responses change. My family's reactions change with time, and maybe at some point I will feel that kind of cathartic release from my mother's constant critical presence in my head, but it has not happened. It's been a little heightened, if anything.

KATIE ROIPHE

Heightened? You still hear her say it, or you just have it in your head?

ALISON BECHDEL

Both. She reads book reviews all day, and she's always excited when she sees a bad one of something. She's got to tell me about it, and I always feel like there's some little implicit message there for me, like, "Be careful." Although when I did actually get a bad review, she was irate on my behalf.

KATIE ROIPHE

So much of this book is about her reaction to this book that it almost feels like we know her reaction to this book. But did she actually give you a satisfying reaction?

ALISON BECHDEL

No. She's maddening. One thing that I really wanted to achieve in this book was to let my mother know how much I loved her. You'd think a person might respond to that by saying, "Thank you," or, "God, that was so moving." I got none of that. I know that she's happy, but only because I know her strange ways: when she's not saying something, I know what she's thinking.

KATIE ROIPHE

Once, my older sister—who's also a writer—said to me that our whole careers could be reduced to those drawings you hang on the refrigerator with magnets when you were a child. And while I resisted this interpretation at the time, it was kind of true. You just want your mother to say that what you did is the most brilliant piece of work, and whatever everyone else says is irrelevant. The *New York Times* . . . who cares?

ALISON BECHDEL

Totally. Your mother would actually do that, though, right?

KATIE ROIPHE

Yeah, my mother puts all the books on the refrigerator with magnets. She might even overmagnetize books, one could argue. But that moment where you're looking for that response and you don't get it is complicated.

ALISON BECHDEL

I write to get from other people the response I didn't get from her. But you are a very prolific writer, and you didn't have that problem. I always think people write out of some deep lack.

KATIE ROIPHE

If you had just this totally well-loved, well-nurtured childhood would you have been that writer, or have been that child creating that beautiful office that you draw with the Dr. Seuss Plexiglas?

ALISON BECHDEL

I think I would be a lawyer now. Not that there's anything wrong with that. But I think that I would just probably not have this anxiety that's always making me make things.

KATIE ROIPHE

As a parent, even if you give your children all the love, they're still going to be tormented and remember that one time you didn't go to their comedy show. You never make your child that secure that they can't become some sort of writer or artist.

ALISON BECHDEL

That's probably true.

KATIE ROIPHE

A lot of the book is about guilt, and writing about your family and grappling with both the compulsion to fight it and the shady impulse, but then the guilt about it. When you finished the book, did you stop feeling guilty?

ALISON BECHDEL

No. I have been racked with guilt and shame ever since I got my copy in the mail. It's been really awful. I had a hard time writing the book. I was very miserable writing it, and I thought I would be released from it when it was published, but it didn't happen. When I got the book I found a billion little tiny mistakes, tiny drawing errors that haunted me. But we don't care about that. Also, I felt I had exposed my mother in a way that she was not really completely on board with.

KATIE ROIPHE

In the final scene you, almost brutally, anatomize all these things that were wrong with the way your mother mothered. And yet, you really generously come out of that, with her having taught you somehow to be an artist. She gave you the way to escape this difficult situation.

ALISON BECHDEL

In many ways my mother kind of threw me overboard, but then she threw me this lifesaver. I feel ridiculous complaining about my mother. She was a pretty good mother. Well, maybe she wasn't. It's such a huge taboo to say anything bad about your mother.

KATIE ROIPHE

Maybe this is what readers are identifying with. She wasn't the worst mother in the world. But, she didn't give you something you really needed. Your mother is like the weather. It's like a storm, a tornado. Perhaps the universal thing here is how those little ways in which someone is a terrible mother hugely affect you. This is something that Winnicott also discusses.

ALISON BECHDEL

He also talked about the "good-enough mother," and most people are so. Certainly my mother was, or I would be psychotic, and I'm not. Pretty much.

KATIE ROIPHE

Are You My Mother? has a lot of scenes in a shrink's office, there's a lot about the person trying to write it, and also a lot about, "How does she really feel about her mother?" Though there are stories in it, the book has so many internal states of mind, parts where nothing at all happens. I'm interested to know how you get those complex internal states on the page. Also, I was thinking about what would this book be without pictures. There are things accomplished in this memoir that you couldn't do if you just had words. How do pictures free you and what do they allow you to do?

ALISON BECHDEL

I feel the reason I am a cartoonist, and why I write visually, is because if I could show you pictures now, I would explain myself better. I can't really think without pictures, and so I will show you some. [Shows a page from the book.] In this scene, I looked at the childhood drawing. I'm examining it, and it reminded me of an illustration in a kids' book. The image keeps leading me. I went and found the picture in the Dr. Seuss book, and, here's the page. I'm looking for this KEEP OUT sign, so I find a picture of the sign. In the text on this page, Dr. Seuss is talking about a Plexiglas dome, which is a phrase I used with my first good therapist to describe my mother's absence and distance. She was sitting in plain sight in the living room, but you couldn't talk to her because she had what seemed like a Plexiglas dome over her head, so I was surprised to find that word in this potent childhood picture book.

As I thought about the Dr. Seuss drawing and looked at it more, I realized it was like a womb. Then I was able to make an analogy to an actual fetus, to me inside of my mother. And this is what that looks like on the page of the book. These images are all linked in a kind of argument, like it's an essay, but the connecting things are images.

KATIE ROIPHE

Finding this thing that leads you to another association is sort of Proustian. If you had an essay, there would be like a million transitions, because we're going from Winnicott to Virginia Woolf to Dr. Seuss. Those transitions would kill you.

ALISON BECHDEL

Sometimes I feel like I could have used more transitions. Sometimes I go back and look at this book and it feels like it's filled with non sequiturs, like it needed a little more something. Of course, I'm not the most accurate or objective reader. I don't have enough distance.

KATIE ROIPHE

Part of what the sheer fact of a picture allows you to do is a kind of simultaneity that cannot be achieved with words. We have to read these in order, one after another, as one does. With pictures and words, and quotes, it's different. In that amazing Dr. Seuss page, you have many different things going on simultaneously, that you telegraph to the reader in this incredibly graceful way. There aren't sixteen thousand people doing what you do. You've created or invented this form that allows for connections that I think are true to life. Like you're sitting there with your girlfriend, and you're having another thought, but how do you show that, if you're doing it in prose?

ALISON BECHDEL

When I first started my book *Fun Home*, I was working with a word processing program, just writing down ideas. I didn't know how else to begin. But I couldn't really get anywhere. I would write and write, and I would hit a dead end. Then I started writing in a drawing program, Adobe Illustrator, and I started to see the page as a two-dimensional field. I visualized where pictures would go and where things would be linked or juxtaposed. But then what happens when I'm just trying to write a sentence—like, if I get asked to do something simple like write a blurb for a book—every sentence or word that I write, I feel like I could go off in eighteen different directions from there. I think that a lot of people feel that way. It's a kind of attention deficit disorder or something. Very good gifted writers can do that just with prose, but in my case pictures enable me to do several things at once, and that's what I'm trying to do.

KATIE ROIPHE

Writers can do it, but it's more clunky.

ALISON BECHDEL

Or it comes across as more experimental. Whereas this, I think this combination with pictures and words is fairly accessible.

KATIE ROIPHE

There's a scene in the book where you're talking to your mother about something important and she's going on about the plumber and the pipes. There's something about this way of representing what's going on in your head, and its contrast, that one can't do in prose in quite the same way. Is there something about this medium that you've created that lends itself to the way people think or remember? Perhaps this is why people identify with your books? Is there something you're capturing about the way actual memory works and the way a family works? Like, you're thinking this, but you're saying this, in a very graphic way.

ALISON BECHDEL

I don't know a lot about neuroscience. For some reason, I find all that kind of boring. Does memory function in a purely visual way? I don't know, but I feel it's a way to access stuff in a deep, immediate way. It took me a long time to get comfortable with a way of drawing my family members. It was hard to do, but just the simple act gave me a weird kind of access to them. Having to externalize them, to draw them, to touch them, was kind of interesting.

KATIE ROIPHE

It's almost hard to see your parents, actually, hard to see what they look like, because you have so many fantasies and weird feelings about them that you don't see them. As a child what your parents look like is very confusing.

ALISON BECHDEL

Plus they're changing anyhow.

KATIE ROIPHE

And you have a huge stretch of time. So you had trouble finding them, but then you found them.

ALISON BECHDEL

I found a way to draw them, a shorthand that seemed to resonate.

Going back to your question about the internal states of mind, I think comics traditionally have been very action-oriented. They are perfectly designed for that, in the same way film is. You see stuff happening. But in a movie, except in a weird experimental one, it's harder to get the same sense of interiority, or immersion in a person's consciousness. I've been trying to get comics to go more inside, to be able to convey subjective experience more.

When comics first started getting taken seriously, Charles McGrath wrote a piece in the *New York Times Magazine* about how comics can be literature. He said that one thing comics aren't great at is lyrical emotion, or nuanced feelings. I forget how he put it, but I felt kind of excited by that. I took it as a challenge. I thought I wanted to figure out how to make comics do that.

KATIE ROIPHE

I don't think a lot of people would be able to read a book that had all this Winnicott and all this Virginia Woolf and was so *thinky*, except that you brought this dynamic form to it. Maybe you brought a little of the Superman to the psychological struggle. The comic seems to have brought action to the externalization of interior states. It would be harder if you tried to write this in prose. Because how much can we read about someone sitting in the psychiatrist's office? You nevertheless managed to bring action to a subject that doesn't inherently have it. Perhaps the form is what brought this kind of Superman-jumping-over-tall-buildings to this subject and made it dynamic, and, as you said, accessible.

ALISON BECHDEL

Maybe I did. I like that.

Questions from the Audience

I'm curious to hear a little more about how you start writing something. Do you visualize it first? Is it like a story? What does it look like? Then, in terms of your process of creating, is it a visual process of drawing something out, or it's more about thinking it through?

ALISON BECHDEL

With Adobe Illustrator, I have a little grid. It's a template, where I can make any combination of panel outlines, so I'm already thinking about what the page is going to look like. I can just start typing on the page. I draw a little text box and start typing with my digital font. It's really a wonderful, flexible way to write. I can change the layout really quickly without having to erase stuff or throw it away.

I'm always thinking very much about the space of the page. There's always a battle between the words and the pictures. This sentence here would be fine, if I were writing prose, but, if I can make it a little shorter, I can get an extra eighth of an inch for the drawing. As I'm writing, I'm also thinking about what's going to go in these boxes. I'm not just like making random choices. I can't even explain what I'm thinking. I somehow know there's going to be a picture there, and I have a rough idea of what it is, but I don't actually draw it. I might do little *sketches.*

Then I print that page out. Once I get it written to my satisfaction, I start sketching right on the page; it's really, really rough at first. I do a lot of posing for all the different characters in the book, or I use family snapshots. I use all the visual research to refine the drawings. Once I have my really good pencil sketch, I then ink it, put into Photoshop, color. I shade it on a separate piece of paper, which I also scan into Photoshop, then stick those all together. I never know what it's going to look like until this moment when I put all the layers together, and then add the text.

Are the looks of the characters different from the real-life people?

ALISON BECHDEL

Well, I tried really, really hard to make them true to life, true to my experience. It's my experience of my mother. I'm sure she doesn't really identify completely with the person I've created, but I didn't try to disguise anyone, or change them. I was trying really hard to get the real people.

I wondered if maybe the characters took off on you.

ALISON BECHDEL

Oh. No. I didn't let them. Often I say there's not really any difference between fiction and nonfiction, it's just whether you call people by the same names or not. But that is a really big difference. It would have been really interesting to let my mother take off on her own as a character. Maybe I'll do that in my next book.

You said there were moments when you were questioning whether the self-referential aspect of writing the story got too intense. How did you balance out that? How did you think about it while you were doing it? The exercise of trying to capture your own consciousness while you are writing might become very complex. How did you figure that out?

ALISON BECHDEL

You're asking how did I balance the intense self-referential element of the story, in a way that wasn't completely overwhelming for the reader. I don't know if I did. I was actually teaching a comics class last spring, and one of the books we read was my book, and I think some of these college kids found it a little too self-reflexive. Perhaps that's because they're young, and not that self-reflexive, they haven't thought about their lives long enough.

KATIE ROIPHE

Didn't you undercut that with a little bit of humor? The book is very funny at certain key points, and that's what cuts against that feeling of, "I'm actually in someone's head." Laughter creates air on the page.

ALISON BECHDEL

I tried to do that.

KATIE ROIPHE

I would say you *did* do it, and it might be self-referential, but that aspect of it is what resonates with a lot of people. If you're trying to grapple with your difficult mother, you're going to have layers of whatever going on. The fact that you're tracking all that and still observing it is very helpful for the rest of us.

ALISON BECHDEL

It was very confusing, though.

KATIE ROIPHE

Did you try to use the humor in that way? Since you look so bewildered, it seems that you didn't.

ALISON BECHDEL

I try not to get too conscious about humor. I get nervous even talking about being funny, because I worry then that I'll never be able to do it. I think that my book *Fun Home* was funnier. This one has a different feel. It's not really very funny, and most of the funny lines are just things that I wrote down that my mother said.

How did you work out the structure of the story?

ALISON BECHDEL

Well, at one point I had this huge six-by-four-foot chart on my wall with hundreds of little Post-its, and index cards, and notes, and a grid. It was a very unwieldy story to write, mostly because there was no story. I had to find a story in all these different strands. At a certain point, I realized that there were actually through-lines. There was the story of my mother's life, going to college in the fifties, and getting married in the sixties. There was my fixation with Donald Winnicott. There was a relationship I had in my twenties. These layers of things that were starting to become clear. It wasn't really an outline, it was just this kind of evolving Excel spreadsheet. I had it on my computer as well as on the wall.

KATIE ROIPHE

It sounds like you're very organized about your research and your creative process. It's not like you just sit there and do it.

ALISON BECHDEL

It's really organized and really belabored. I wish it just came out of me, but that didn't happen.

What was the process of writing this book like compared with writing Fun Home*?*

ALISON BECHDEL

In the review by Heather Love that I mentioned at the beginning, she talks about some people who have criticized *Are You My Mother?* for being shapeless, for not having a conventional narrative. She says that *Fun Home* was like a classical temple, built over Minoan ruins, and that *Fun Home* is about an Oedipal struggle. That book was about a pretty straightforward battle with my dad, but the story with me and my mother is pre-Oedipal. That's where the drama with the mother happens, in these early years, these really murky inaccessible years, the same period which Donald Winnicott shed so much light on. It is necessarily a less linear kind of story. So maybe out of necessity this book is more complicated.

Winnicott also said a really cool thing: "The father must be murdered, but the mother can be dismantled." I keep wanting to say it the other way. I kind of want to say, "The father *can* be murdered, but the mother *must be* dismantled," because it's a lot easier to murder someone than to dismantle them, as I discovered.

How do you get through to the end of something when it's so difficult, so emotionally painful? Even if you love writing and drawing, this particular writing and drawing project is excruciating.

ALISON BECHDEL

It helps to have a publisher breathing down your neck. I was way late on this book. It took me a couple years past the deadline I had promised, and that was nerve-racking. I was living through all these experiences of shame and rejection and humiliation. I was steeped in that stuff all day, for years, and it was compounded by the fact that I was going through menopause, which no one should talk about. No one is interested in that unless you are one of the people who are at this moment going through it, so I won't talk about that anymore.

KATIE ROIPHE

Was there a moment where you had a revelation, where you were going to put the difficulty of the process into the book itself? Was there a moment where you thought, "I'm going to put my struggle about writing this book into the book itself," or did you always intend to put it in?

ALISON BECHDEL

It was not part of the original conception at all. At the start I didn't put it in. But I did have an idea at the very beginning that the book would be about writing *Fun Home*, about writing the memoir about my father, and my agent said I could not do that, she thought that nobody would have the patience for that. She felt it was just too self-indulgent. So, I avoided it. I didn't do it for a couple years. Instead I worked on this other version of the book, but when I finally showed that to my agent, she thought it did not make sense. I then went back to my original idea, and made the book about writing the other book, and then all of my process and difficulties about writing this book became a part of it, too, and I just let it happen.

KATIE ROIPHE

And once you had that, did it make it easier to write it?

ALISON BECHDEL

No. At least I felt like I was going to finish it at that point, but it wasn't great. The only moment of true pleasure and inspiration was one day when I envisioned Virginia Woolf and Donald Winnicott meeting in the park. That just came out of nowhere.

KATIE ROIPHE

Did you have a moment when you looked at this book and thought it was great and that you were happy it came out this way? Have you had some untormented moment of satisfaction with this book?

ALISON BECHDEL

I felt really good about it a couple of months when I was finishing the drawing, when my life was turned over to drawing, like twenty hours a day. But then it ended. When I saw the actual book it went away.

I wanted to ask you about the use of color in your books.

ALISON BECHDEL

When I was writing *Fun Home*, my original idea was to make it just black-and-white as a kind of defiant act to my father, who was very obsessed with color. I wanted to prove that you could tell a nuanced story in black-and-white. I became a cartoonist so I didn't have to deal with color. Later on, talking to the art department, we realized there was a way to get a very cool effect by turning my gray ink-wash shade to green. I am glad I did that, I think it's very cool.

With *Are You My Mother?*, I liked working with just two

colors, with black and then another color, so I kept doing that, so I just had to pick a different color. Red was pretty much the only other color there was.

How do you deal with the frustration of, supposedly, writing non-fiction about your real family and the real conversations with your mother, and not having a recording of everything?

ALISON BECHDEL

I hate that. I wish I had a video camera on my shoulder all the time, but that would become impossible, because you don't have time to watch it. I'm getting to feel a little more confident and free in reconstructing things like conversations I had when I was three. I try not to do that too much, but you kind of have to do that. I wish I had transcripts of the actual conversations, but it is a little frustrating that I don't.

You are very personal in what you write, and very willing to expose yourself, like draw yourself having sex, and in the bathroom, and you just tell the truth. But there's also this other element where I sense you're a very deeply private person. I was led to think so after I saw a drawing you did of yourself having to give yourself a pep talk, before giving some chocolates for Christmas to the staff in the post office. You had to psych yourself up just to do that little thing. I want to ask about the coexistence of these two contradictory impulses of wanting to be seen and wanting to be invisible at the same time.

ALISON BECHDEL

How do I reconcile the fact that I show all these very personal moments from my life, with the fact that I'm basically almost autistic shy? Of course you wouldn't know that because I do pretty good sitting in public. I'm functioning pretty well.

I don't know. Being my public self, I feel like I've created this almost character that I can hide behind. I think it's accurate. I think it's me. But it's still like an avatar. But when I'm just trying to give the ladies at the bank a Christmas present, I'm just paralyzed with shyness and anxiety. But that's because I'm not talking about myself.

KATIE ROIPHE

A lot of writers are shy, because the way that they can express themselves is in writing, and they can't be comfortable in a room. So they compensate in these elaborate ways.

ALISON BECHDEL

Now we always have to go out in public and talk like this. Virginia Woolf didn't have to. Imagine if she'd had to go on an author's tour.

7

Blake Bailey
&
D. T. Max

D. T. MAX

Blake started off working on Richard Yates, who has had this intense, small readership. He's a writer's writer. Then he moved on to John Cheever, a mid-century American fictional icon. So I presume he, like all the rest of us mere mortals, was looking around for another project, and came upon Charles Jackson. At first I thought he'd come upon Shirley Jackson, but it was Charles. Why?

BLAKE BAILEY

Why Charlie Jackson?

D. T. MAX

Yes, make your case for him.

BLAKE BAILEY

I have long been a great admirer of his novel *The Lost Weekend*. I read it first in college, and I've read it five or six times since then. The great portrait of an alcoholic in American literature remains, and perhaps will forever remain, Don Birnam. He was aptly characterized, in one of the reviews at the time, as a mixture of Hamlet and Mr. Toad from *The Wind in the Willows*.

I was completely fried after writing those two cinder-block literary biographies [Yates and Cheever]. I wanted to do something more modest. I thought about doing this sort of Lytton Strachey-esque *Portraits in Miniature* about failed, forgotten writers, because I kept tripping across them in my research on Cheever and Yates.

D. T. MAX

Who were some of them?

BLAKE BAILEY

Flannery Lewis, Calvin Kentfield, Nathan Asch . . .

D. T. MAX

When you said "Flannery" I was with you, but then you said "Lewis," and I was like, no.

BLAKE BAILEY

Like I threw you this big curveball, right? Well, these three writers were considered real up-and-comers in their day. Flannery Lewis published something like three novels in three years. He peed in the fountain at Yaddo and was thrown out personally by Elizabeth Ames. They were all wild and prolific guys. Talented guys. But now you can hardly Google them. They are gone. It's like they never existed. And I thought this was fascinating.

Why do some people make it? There's this oral biography of Hemingway, *The True Gen*, and Nathan Asch, who died all the way back in 1964, was interviewed. He knew Hemingway. They were both in Paris in the twenties. And he spoke ruefully about him, sort of, "I was talented, and Hemingway was talented. But he made it, and I didn't." He talked about how Hemingway, the young Hemingway, would walk down the street in the Montparnasse, and he shed light as he passed by, like Richard Cory, I guess, in Edwin Arlington Robinson's poem. He was so charismatic. He was so charming. He had that smile, you know. And so everyone reads Hemingway. Nathan Asch was sort of this little nebbish guy, and he's nowhere.

D. T. MAX

That's what got you started?

BLAKE BAILEY

I was interested in that idea, so I thought, who remembers Charles Jackson? And he had written this wonderful novel, a classic in its time. I went back to my dog-eared copy of *The Lost Weekend*. I had the 1963 version, the Time Reading Program reprint, and I read what the editors of *Time* had written in the preface. It said something like, "Charles Jackson is now chairman of the New Brunswick, New Jersey, AA chapter, and he's sober, and he's the doting father of two daughters," and so on. That sounded like a nice sort of redemptive fable story.

D. T. MAX

That's what you were looking for?

BLAKE BAILEY

Right after, I Googled him and found out he had died of an overdose at the Chelsea Hotel in 1968, and was living with a Czechoslovakian laborer named Stanley Zednik. What had happened to the family man? What about the sobriety? I thought there was a story there.

I got in touch with the daughters, who were guarded, but very kind, and courteous, and helpful. They directed me to Dartmouth College, where there were like twenty boxes of Jackson's papers in the basement. Among these papers I found three hundred pages of letters from Jackson and his wife Rhoda to Charlie's brother, Boom, so I read those first.

I'm not quite sure how many people in this room have read *The Lost Weekend* or how many have watched the movie. But if you have seen it, you may recall the apartment where Don, the main character, lives with his brother, Wick. It turns out that that apartment in the movie is an exact replica of the apartment that Charles shared with his brother Fred, called Boom, on East Fifty-fifth Street, in the mid-1930s. That was the time when Charlie was at the worst of his alcoholism, and his brother was trying to get him back on his feet again. It was very much the same situation that you had in *The Lost Weekend*.

D. T. MAX

What else did you find?

BLAKE BAILEY

I also found the original typescript of *The Lost Weekend*, which Charlie had given to Dartmouth in 1949. So it'd been there for a long time.

I read the letters. And those three hundred pages confirmed everything that was in *The Lost Weekend*. Charlie had been a mess, and he'd also struggled with pill addiction later on in his life. Boom, his brother, became very frustrated with him. The letters sort of taper off in the late fifties, something that suggests that at that point Boom was sick of Charlie's messing up. Rhoda comes across as very long-suffering, but very devoted, too, because Charlie was the kindest, sweetest of men. And when he was sober, he was a wonderful husband and father. His daughters adore him to this day.

The letters to Boom were so fascinating that I began to look at the other boxes. They were a treasure trove. I found practically every letter that Jackson had written as an adult, to Judy Garland, to Thomas Mann . . .

D. T. MAX

At that point, you decided that he would be the subject of your next biography?

BLAKE BAILEY

It was a fascinating story, a mystery to be solved. How did he go from sobriety, and why did he stop writing? He did not publish a novel from 1948 to 1967. What was he doing in between? At some point I even thought he became a used-car salesman, because I found a book called *How to Buy a Used Car*, by Charles R. Jackson, but it turned out it wasn't *the* Charles Jackson, even though the middle initial was the same. Anyway, he went nearly twenty years without publishing a novel, and then the novel that he did publish, the year before his death, made the *New York Times* bestseller list. Charlie was still famous in those days, and so when the author of *The Lost Weekend* came back out of nowhere to publish this, it became a big event and the book did really well. After it came out, he was interviewed by Barbara Walters on *The Today Show.* It was a great story. I had a ball working on it.

D. T. MAX

If you were to make a case for the fiction by Charles Jackson besides *The Lost Weekend*, what would you send us to read?

BLAKE BAILEY

The two books that have just been reissued by Vintage, very much at my behest. That is, his first book of short stories, *The Sunnier Side*, which critics just raved about at the time. It was one of the most reviewed books of 1950. And the *New York Times* did a little sidebar about it, explaining that of the fifty-seven major reviewers that reviewed it, only five wrote negative reviews. That's huge! The book was regarded as the latter-day equivalent of Sherwood Anderson's *Winesburg, Ohio*.

D. T. MAX

For those of us who have a literary-historical mind-set, where would you put Charles Jackson in terms of American letters? In other words, who does he connect to? What traditions is he writing out of? Does he leave any descendants?

BLAKE BAILEY

That is a very difficult question to answer. *The Lost Weekend*, especially in its early couple of chapters, has what we critics would call a Wavian quality. He writes like the early comic novels of Evelyn Waugh. Don Birnam is a sort of Chaplinesque character, stumbling from one calamity to another, and there is a sort of a funny, picaresque quality to him. Part of the book's genius is the way that those early, kind of Wavian chapters grade into horror, in the latter part of the book. You almost don't notice it happening. Charles Jackson acknowledges a debt to Waugh. But there is a black, surreal zaniness to *The Lost Weekend* that one also finds in [Nathanael West's] *Miss Lonelyhearts* and *The Day of the Locust*. But I think it's sort of an affinity of the cultural ethos.

D. T. MAX

He didn't read Nathanael West, though.

BLAKE BAILEY

There is no evidence that he ever read him. Nathanael West died before *The Lost Weekend* was published, so he probably didn't read Charles Jackson, either.

D. T. MAX

The first review that has come out for your Charles Jackson biography is a rave from Adam Kirsch, writing in the *Wall Street Journal*. The headline is "A Great American Biography." Playfully and charmingly, the review posits the following axiom for biography: "Common sense suggests that the better a writer is, the more he deserves to have his story told, but it is precisely the genius's genius that no biographer can explain, or usually even evoke." And therefore, by implication, somewhere along this continuum, the worse the writer, the more room there is for great biography. I wonder if you agree or disagree with this.

BLAKE BAILEY

I think there are nuances to what Adam actually said that eluded your paraphrase.

D. T. MAX

But do you agree with that? Is that something you thought going into Charles Jackson? Sort of, if I do some immortal genius, then there's no room for me.

BLAKE BAILEY

No. First of all, he basically says, Charles Jackson was *not* a genius, like Cheever, arguably, like Yates, and certainly like Philip Roth. He was just an above-average guy who dreamed of being a genius. But no, that's not the mystery I was trying to solve. The mystery I was trying to solve was how did the near-genius who wrote *The Lost Weekend* write such pedestrian books later? And you can almost not recognize the author of *The Lost Weekend* in most of the work that followed, albeit not all of it. The short answer for why Jackson never equaled the achievement of *The Lost Weekend* is because he was always stoned when he was writing his later work. He wrote *The Lost Weekend* cold sober. He'd been sober for almost eight years, and that was his talent, that was Charles Jackson when he was on the beam. He was freaked out by the success of *The Lost Weekend*, and, let me emphasize, we tend to forget that it was a huge hit. It's been so overshadowed by the movie, but it sold half a million copies. It was in the Modern Library. It was turned into a comic strip, a syndicated comic strip. You know you've made it when—

D. T. MAX

But it was booted out of the Modern Library.

BLAKE BAILEY

Only because of Bennett Cerf.

D. T. MAX

Who knew that?

BLAKE BAILEY

Well, Bennett Cerf had been courting Charlie Jackson for years to come away from Farrar and Rinehart to Random House, and when the time came, Charlie did leave Farrar and Rinehart—which was then Rinehart and Company—because Farrar had joined up with Roger Straus, so he followed him to Farrar and Straus. Bennett Cerf retaliated by yanking *The Lost Weekend* from the Modern Library and replacing it with *Little Women*. That's tough.

D. T. MAX

Why isn't there room for both of them?

BLAKE BAILEY

You didn't really follow that previous thought to the end, so may I do so? Charlie was completely freaked out by his own success. He had Edmund Wilson raving about him, and he was like, "What am I going to do now? I'm just this misfit from the sticks, little Newark, New York, twenty miles from Lake Ontario, where they thought I was a goofball"—and a sissy, I might add. So it freaked him out, and he was totally blocked. He found the only way to get unblocked was to take Seconal, to take tranquilizers.

I found medical notes from his doctor, who wasn't even a psychiatrist. It was this doctor who treated him in Hanover, New Hampshire, Dr. Sven Gundersen, who also treated Robert Frost. A pulmonary specialist. But he was the one. Charlie liked him, so he would go to Mary Hitchcock Hospital and dry out whenever he overdosed, or went on a bender, or what have you. Gundersen wrote, "Mr. Jackson is addicted to Seconal." They're reds. They're tranquilizers. Serious tranquilizers. And Gundersen added, "Seconal is a powerful tranquilizer, however, oddly enough, it has the reverse effect on Mr. Jackson." When Charlie took it, he would become *galvanized*, he'd soar, and just suddenly the thoughts would be rushing in and he'd be writing them on paper.

I don't know if any of you here are fiction writers, but it is axiomatic: you do not try to write fiction when you're drunk or stoned. It's always terrible. John Cheever knew that. Cheever was taking his first drink of the morning earlier and earlier, until he was sneaking into the pantry for a scoop of gin at nine o'clock in the morning. But that simply meant that he had to wrap up the writing at eight forty-five. It did not mean that he would get the scoop of gin and then go write. He knew better.

Now, Charlie loved the idea of being a celebrated writer. Don Birnam, his character, has all these fantasies of being not only a genius writer, but also a genius actor, and a genius piano player, and all that. That's Charlie. So he had to play out the role of the writer, and if that meant being addicted to Seconal most of his adult life, that's what he had to do. But he did not write a single published word after *The Lost Weekend* that was not written under the influence of tranquilizers.

D. T. MAX

What about *The Sunnier Side*?

BLAKE BAILEY

Two of its best stories, "Palm Sunday" and "Rachel's Summer," were written in 1939, when he was still sober, before he'd even written *The Lost Weekend*. And they're pioneering. Charlie was a completely autobiographical writer, and "Palm Sunday" is a totally true story about how he was molested by the choirmaster in his small town, when he was fourteen. "Rachel's Summer" is about his older sister, Thelma, getting hit by the train. Charlie's sister and brother were killed by a train when he was thirteen, and in the small town of Newark, New York, rather than comforting the family, they instead spread a rumor that Thelma had been pregnant at the time she died and that God in his infinite wisdom had taken her before the disgrace became obvious. This rumor blighted Charlie's mother's life for the rest of her years.

D. T. MAX

I'm wondering what makes a good subject for a biography. If there were a biographer-in-the-making out here, what would you tell him or her to look for?

BLAKE BAILEY

The prerequisite of writing a literary biography is, make sure you admire the work. If you don't, you're going to waste a lot of your time on miserable labor, and it's excruciating. You've got to be obsessive to write a decent biography. As you may have noticed, I'm wired pretty tight, so, I'm the man for the job. One needs to admire the work, and have a good story.

Charlie was a great story. Here's a man who wrote a novel of genius. He never equaled the achievement, but he never stopped trying. In the meantime, he got into one horrific scrape after another. He got tuberculosis. He had this closeted gay mentor who made sure that he and his gorgeous bother, also gay, named Boom, lived a life of luxury in Davos, Switzerland. This was Bronson Winthrop, a big Wall Street lawyer, the partner of Henry Stimson, who was the Secretary of War in FDR's cabinet. He was fabulously wealthy, erudite, and cultured, and Charlie was his protégé, and he was a closeted gay man.

D. T. MAX

You think there was no romantic involvement between Bronson Winthrop and either of the brothers?

BLAKE BAILEY

No. Bronson Winthrop was a big fan of Plato.

D. T. MAX

That's what they all say.

BLAKE BAILEY

That *is* what they all say! Bronson's father, Egerton—the subject of a celebrated portrait by Sargent—was Edith Wharton's best friend. And Bronson had this gallery of pictures of his protégés over the years, but Charlie insisted that he was the most innocent man he'd ever met. Now, Boom, his brother, definitely stirred Bronson. Charlie had the platonic, intellectual friendship with him, and Bronson saw Boom and said, "I'd like to sublimate my passion for *that*." I have a gorgeous picture of Boom in my book that you should check out.

D. T. MAX

Since you are an unusually productive biographer, I'd like to talk about your processes. One senses very little time is wasted, despite the carpools with the eight-year-old daughter, and taking the beagle for a walk. If I have this right, you've said that you take three pages of single-spaced notes, and turn it into two pages of finished prose. Tell us a little about that.

BLAKE BAILEY

What do you do?

D. T. MAX

I have no such equation, so I'm really curious. Is there a way that you accumulate your notes first, so you have this incredibly beautiful sort of pile of a book-in-waiting, and you begin to write it out of a complete stack of notes?

BLAKE BAILEY

Yes, when you're done with your research, after however many years, your computer is ready to explode with undifferentiated data that you need to put in order, so I go and I lie down on my very comfortable couch—I have a very comfortable couch in my study, since you asked. And I don't allow myself to look at anything, or consult anything. And I've got my legs over the beagle, because she loves that. Then I write down all the major episodes of my subject's life. And if it doesn't occur to me off the top of my head, it's not worth writing down. I fill up a legal pad, and then I type that up, and then I cut-and-paste, and start thinking about structure. Do I want to be strictly chronological? No. I want it to be thematic and *semi*-chronological. I want to talk about the alcoholism here, and I want to talk about his doting relationship with his daughters here, and this incident attaches nicely to this theme, and—blah, blah.

After about a year, I have a rough structure, and I'm

starting to plug stuff in. I call it "rough structure," but it's extremely complex by then. I'm plugging in the research, plugging in, plugging in. Say I've interviewed a couple hundred people, and I have five versions of one anecdote. I take the best line from each, this person told it best. And as you're going along, you're throwing stuff out, winnowing, winnowing. The structure is refining itself. Finally, after about two years of working on the outline, I have absolutely every line in place. I have, say, seven hundred pages of single-spaced notes. I know exactly how the book is laid out, and I can start writing. Producing two double-spaced pages of finished prose a day is tough, but if you've got your notes in order, it's completely doable.

D. T. MAX

So you're able to sit there at a certain moment and say you're two-thirds of the way through the writing of your biography.

BLAKE BAILEY

I can calculate mathematically how many days I have before I'm finished.

D. T. MAX

So when your daughter asks when will you be done, you can actually give an answer?

BLAKE BAILEY

June 14th.

D. T. MAX

Do you ever find that you've collected notes on a part of the writer's life that doesn't interest you much?

BLAKE BAILEY

Yes. The only real problem I encounter once I have my notes is when I realize that I don't really have to include certain bits. I feel like this part is superfluous—and that's great. And this sometimes means that I finish the three pages, or whatever, *early* that day, and I only need to write a single paragraph. So I've done my allotment, and I can take a walk or go to a movie.

D. T. MAX

We spoke of Charles Jackson as the exception, in regards to the rest of the writers you have written about, but let's look at it from a different point of view. We have in Richard Yates an anguished, alcoholic, middle-aged writer with possible bisexual tendencies.

BLAKE BAILEY

I wouldn't agree with bisexual. I kind of vacillated about that, but didn't put it in the book.

D. T. MAX

The reviewers did. You don't think that's true?

BLAKE BAILEY

That Yates had bisexual tendencies? I think he was terrified of being perceived as a sissy because he was a mama's boy. He had this drunken, overprotective mother. His childhood was a nightmare, and he clung to her skirt because he had nothing else to cling to, so the rest of his life he played this bogus man's man persona, but I don't think that that necessarily points to the sexual proclivities.

D. T. MAX

All right, I'm going to withdraw the question. I'm going to ask you this one.

BLAKE BAILEY

Which is, "Why do I always write about bisexual men?"

D. T. MAX

No, let me try to rephrase this in a way that will squeak past the biographer's gaze. So you've written about three middle-aged men in anguished—

BLAKE BAILEY

They weren't *always* middle-aged . . .

D. T. MAX

Men in anguished relationship to their prose, heavily alcoholic, and basically blocked. And then comes Philip Roth. How do you fit him into your paradigm?

BLAKE BAILEY

I have no "paradigm" per se. Every writer is a mass of contradictions. Every human being is a mass of contradictions.

D. T. MAX

Philip Roth said to the *New York Times*, "I work for Blake Bailey now." You're giving him a Form 1099 at the end of the year. How did that happen?

BLAKE BAILEY

I found out that Philip and my predecessor, Ross Miller, had called it quits, so I went home and wrote Philip a letter saying, "I'm available. I'm between projects. You remember me. We corresponded about my Cheever book"—because he and Cheever were friends. About a week later I was on a weekend trip with my family, and I was driving over a narrow, rickety bridge on the eastern shore of Virginia, and my brand-new iPhone rang. It said "Blocked," and I thought it was the Obama people, since they'd been calling me incessantly because I'd volunteered for the 2008 campaign, and when they call, it always said "Unknown." My wife insisted that I should keep my eyes on the road, and I said I should take the call since it did not say "Unknown." She snapped the phone out of my hand and said, "Watch the road. We're going to drive off the bridge." So I got back to my bed-and-breakfast and I'm soaking in a tub and I pick up my message and Philip Roth has left a voice message. He has this lovely, sort of sonorous, Murrow-esque voice.

So here's Philip Roth. He got my letter. He wants to talk to me. I immediately try to call him back, and it's one of those Verizon answering services, where it says, "The person you're trying to call is not available. Click." You can't even leave a message for them. So I said to my wife, "Thanks a lot. Now I can't be Philip Roth's biographer." But I went home, and sure enough the phone rang again, and it said "Blocked," and you know I threw myself on the phone, and it was Philip Roth again, and he immediately launches into this story about Charles Jackson. When Roth got out of the Army in 1956 he needed a job, and his brother Sandy was an art director at J. Walter Thompson ad agency, and Charlie was a script editor at *Kraft Television Theatre*, which was produced by J. Walter Thompson. So Philip had an interview with Charlie, and Philip tells me that story. Then he stops, and there's a pensive pause, and he says, "Do you ever write about someone who's still alive and not drunk all the time?" And I said, "No. You'd be my first, and I'd really like to talk about it."

D. T. MAX

But he also admired your work, right? He had read the Cheever.

BLAKE BAILEY

He had read both Cheever *and* Yates, I think.

D. T. MAX

What did he say about them?

BLAKE BAILEY

He liked them, especially the Cheever book.

D. T. MAX

Has he read the Jackson?

BLAKE BAILEY

Yes. He finished it in three days. That's pretty good. And he called me up and said, "Blake, this is really wonderful." But really he was consoling me. "I don't know if it's going to be a big seller, Blake. It's wonderful, and you and I know that, but it's an awfully sad story." To that effect.

D. T. MAX

In reviews of your biographies, it's pointed out that you capture a subject's humanity, humanness, that sort of thing. That obviously requires a sort of act of empathy on your part. You make it sound sort of very dry and technical, but obviously there's an act of a human being encountering another human being going on in your pages.

BLAKE BAILEY

Okay, well, thank you. That's a generously worded question, Dan, and I appreciate it. There's a character in *Exit Ghost*, Philip Roth's *Exit Ghost*, and it's a young would-be literary biographer named Richard Kliman. He wants to write a sort of pathography of E. I. Lonoff, Nathan Zuckerman's revered mentor, and his thesis, Kliman's thesis, is that Lonoff had an incestuous relationship—this is kind of informed by the Henry Roth story—with his half-sister, and that this scandal, this trauma, shaped his whole life and shaped his whole work. Now, this is what Philip hates. He hates tendentiousness. He hates pat generalizations. He hates psychobabble. And this is what a bad biographer does. A bad biographer reaches a general opinion about a subject, just to make it accessible—he's a good man, say, or he's a bad man. It's poisonous.

I gather all the evidence. Everything I can get my hands on. Everyone's testimony, and it is wildly contradictory. I heard things about Cheever from his detractors that would absolutely make your hair stand on end. You take it all, and you sift it, and you find what the themes are. In any human life the themes are multifarious, especially in a writer's life. F. Scott Fitzgerald said there could never be a good biography of a good writer, because he's too many people if he's any good. You have to keep an open mind, because your subject is too contradictory, and you've got to somehow reconcile all those contradictions. Like anyone else, I, too, have my despicable qualities—

D. T. MAX

Your wife is a pain management psychologist.

BLAKE BAILEY

But I am not the sum of my despicable qualities, and in a great artist, despicable qualities tend to be even larger, but so are the virtues.

D. T. MAX

I'm very intrigued by your forthcoming memoir, *The Splendid Things We Planned*. Usually the biographer disappears behind the subject. That's the standard position. We don't know anything about Blake, really, but his biographer will know something about him that's not easy to find—

BLAKE BAILEY

Nobody's going to write a biography of me—no biographers except Strachey, maybe, get their own biographies—so, if people are interested, I hope they'll just read my memoir.

8

Tina Chang & Tracy K. Smith

TRACY K. SMITH

It's so nice to be at the Strand. Tina and I were just talking about how, when we were grad students in New York City, we would spend long days on the ladders downstairs here, looking through the books. So it's really nice to be able to share some work here as well. And Tina and I are dear friends, so it's also a delight to be able to have this conversation. I often preface reading poems from *Life on Mars* by saying that initially I was thinking about the genre of science fiction as a way of looking at America and American life. Of course, I'm a poet, so it put me in a slightly different position. I had a lot of fun watching a lot of science fiction movies from when I was growing up in the seventies and eighties, and thinking about what that genre brought to my own poetic voice. During my work on this manuscript, my father became ill and passed away. It was rather unexpected. I found myself in need of some kind of language to express my grief for that loss. Outer space and the loneliness of it seemed like a good construct for it, so those are some of the notes struck in this book.

TINA CHANG

I tried so hard to be Tracy's opening act, but she wouldn't let me. She's so generous. Tracy and I were on a writing retreat once. In fact, our mentor and teacher Mark Doty was kind enough to offer up his summerhouse at Fire Island. I remember feeling quite terrified and joyful at the same time. Terrified because I was actually sitting in Mark Doty's room writing my book and joyful because Tracy was in the next room writing her book, and I thought: *the only thing separating our ideas is a thin wall.* We were each pregnant with our first child—not together; separately. It felt like there was creation happening all around us. Tracy is the type of person who writes her poems and then comes out looking incredibly radiant, as if she'd just gone through a sauna. She's incredibly open about sharing her poems. I remember how grateful I was for that almost childlike openness she had about sharing her work so soon after the making of it. It was an incredibly special time for me and I feel grateful for it. So these books were written in tandem. But there are so many things I don't know about your process. What were some of the invisible elements of process that were influencing you?

TRACY K. SMITH

That's a hard question. When I think about that time, I feel like it was a very spiritual time. I think loss and expectation push us to a place where we're trying to imagine what we have no access to, or no literal access to, or no proof of. I remember trying to find the voices that felt like maybe they had gotten close to it, and one of the poets is Lucille Clifton. We were both students of hers when we were at Columbia, and I remember she would tell us stories about poems that she kind of received, that she imagined were, or understood to be, voices speaking to or through her. Those poems later appeared in *Mercy*, one of her last books. I always envied that. I always believed that maybe the work of a poet is to learn how to listen, not just to ourselves, not just to what we know or what our sense of language can guide us to, but to truly being receptive to everything around us. I wanted to do that, not only because I like that idea but because I was trying to say goodbye to my father. I'd lost my mother fourteen years before, and I felt like losing him opened up a more mature sense of closure, or an opportunity for that for me. So, as I was working on the book, I was thinking about the events in the world that were troubling me and wanting to find a way that they might teach me what question might be worth asking. I don't know that any of the poems get anywhere near an answer, but wanting to isolate events and questions felt productive to me. Somehow, I aligned that impulse close to the poems. The poems are asking questions about where my father might have gone, what space I might try and listen toward or imagine in terms of him, in order to maintain a connection.

TINA CHANG

When you were thinking about these things, what was the first poem you wrote where these larger questions started to come into being?

TRACY K. SMITH

There's a poem in the book called "It and Company." The first version of it felt very blasphemous to me. It was called "Straight Talk." It was a poem in my mind that was angrily addressed at God, the God I had grown up with. It's a poem that ends "unconvinced by our zeal, it is unappeasable." But the original pronoun was *you*, and I remember during that time I had a lot of time to wake up and sit down and write, and that honesty opened up a different space in my imagination. I think later the frustration with this idea of God became productive in pushing to try to actively enlarge or disrupt the sense of the creator or the source that just seemed too remote to me.

I wanted to ask you something. I'm so fascinated by the way that 9/11 figured into your description of some of the poems and your process. I believe, and I wonder if you feel this way, too, that so many American poets, particularly people of our generation, changed in terms of our sense of what a poem might do after that catastrophe. I know everything changed, the whole world changed, and our vocabulary as citizens changed. I feel like that event, and the way we've been reeling from it ever since, has opened up a space for the world to come into the work that I think in the eighties or nineties, when we were younger, seemed taboo—in fact, seemed impossible without sacrificing the lyrical. My question has a couple of strains. One thing I feel is really magical about your work is that those concerns are projected onto a future that is very deeply linked to history and to mythology. It also, as you describe, has a corollary in a private realm, so the speakers of the poems are often dealing with some kind of upheaval or struggle that seems parallel to something that might be broader or more public. Can you talk about how you got to the vocabulary for that? Was it something you were searching for?

TINA CHANG

When I started writing the book, and this was before 9/11, I felt as if a lot of my concerns felt domestic. My language centered around love, and my world felt quite small. Then, after 9/11, there was something that shifted for me, as it did for many people. I had a profound realization—it shouldn't have *been* profound—that things could happen here on our soil. It was something that a poet who I admire greatly, Carolyn Forché, talked about so often in her work. How could I have admired this woman so much, and have followed her work throughout my lifetime, and only be making this realization now? I think it was around that time that my vocabulary shifted. I was editing an anthology for about ten years, *Language for a New Century*, and as I was sifting through and reading poems from around the world and poring over them, my sense of language changed and expanded. I was fascinated by what the lyric could do, and not understanding it right away, but feeling it through the texture and fabric of another language, and then seeing it translated into English was transformative. I felt like all of that was very deeply a part of learning about my own limitless language.

Were there particular poems that were more difficult for you to write than others in the book?

TRACY K. SMITH

Oh, yeah. There's one poem that I don't think I've ever read. I'll back up a little bit. I gave a reading a few nights ago and my father's girlfriend of twelve years was visiting New York. She was in the audience as I was reading some of the elegies for him. Suddenly, knowing that he wasn't just a character to everyone else in the room but me, but that there was someone who had shared her life with him, I felt very vulnerable and I also felt very grateful that maybe I was invoking him somehow that might be realer than when I read those poems to strangers. But there are some poems in the book about family that are a little bit hard. There's a poem called "No Fly Zone" that is addressed to someone in my family who I have tremendous love for and also a desire to push in some way. I feel like that is a poem that I'm still not sure that the impulse behind it is right. It made me say some things that I always tried to swallow.

TINA CHANG

I remember one of the poems you read to me when we were away on our retreat, and I remember that you felt differently about the poem than I did. I felt like it was really reaching that place of pure vulnerability. I was so surprised when you read that poem, and I thought it was really something profound in the making.

Questions from the Audience

Why poetry?

TRACY K. SMITH

I remember the moment that I *got* poetry. I had always loved it as a child. I loved making puzzles with words, and I liked the feeling of wisdom that I attributed to poems and I wanted that for myself. But when I was older and in college, reading a poem and really coming under its spell, I realized that it was visceral and that it afforded the reader the opportunity to stop and look at very small details with such scrutiny that they become completely other. The poem that really did that for me was Seamus Heaney's "Digging," in which the poet, the speaker, is looking at a pen, and at the beginning of the poem he compares the pen to a gun. He then considers the pen and his environment, and goes backward in time and remembers his father and grandfather working the land, and by the end of the poem he's stepped back into that history and that sense of place and he looks at the pen and compares it to a tool one can dig with. And so suddenly, the pen becomes a completely different kind of implement, but it also suggests a different kind of urgency, and a different kind of location, and that just blew my mind. I wanted to be able to look at the things that were at hand and let them teach me something, not just about myself but about the world I was in. What about you?

TINA CHANG

I feel like I get asked that question a lot since serving as Poet Laureate of Brooklyn, maybe in slightly different ways each time. I think it's an important question. I find that when I watch children, and I have had the opportunity to go to quite a few public and private schools, I've noticed that their tendency is to go toward what Robert Hass talks about as the "rhythmic imagination." Even my son, who is three, now likes to write poems. There's something to be said that the creative imagination works toward a kind of song.

When Tracy and I were going to Columbia together, we had a wonderful teacher named Alfred Corn. He was a very, very smart man and his lessons were very intimidating to me. He would make us read poems with a Shakespearean rhythm that I didn't think I could master, and I was laughing at myself all the time. But now, when I look back on this education, I remember his main lesson began with rhythm. We begin with heartbeat. I think that we grow up knowing that, and then at one point something changes somewhere in our education of poetry and we have a tendency to become a little bit intimidated by it, but if you reach back and think about when we were children and how our imagination was alive and it grew with poetry, you realize that it's not really that far away. If you think about the more profound occasions in our lives like funerals or weddings, it's always the poem that seems to be the document or the statement or song that is just the right expression that encapsulates the urgency of the moment. One of the first poems that I ever understood was T. S. Eliot's "Love Song of J. Alfred Prufrock." It was the famous first few lines that got me; I wondered *what* is this patient upon a table and *why* is it compared to the sky? That kind of questioning made me love poetry, because I wanted to understand that natural curiosity that I had. So I think it's that inquiry that keeps me excited and encourages me to wonder.

TRACY K. SMITH

I feel like the language that we live in is so disruptive to the kinds of insights that we are not necessarily able to paraphrase. We live in the language of text and commerce and a poem is designed to bring us closer to the language of ecstatic experience. I'm not saying this in a religious way, but it's language that is willing to perform those impossible feats. I know many people are required to read poetry in school, and it becomes an adversarial undertaking in understanding what the poet is trying to say. But I wish that there were equal space in our lives for the language of poetry.

You have to depersonalize your poetry to get to your eventual art form. How do you recognize that emotion? Is it more to do with form or more with how you feel?

TINA CHANG

There are so many ways to approach that. You ask any poet and it's slightly different. I remember reading an interview with Sharon Olds and the interviewer is asking her how she begins her poem, where does a poem live? Where does it begin? Where is the seed? For her it was sound, and she said whenever she begins writing in her notebooks, she begins with sound. I begin with an image. The image has always been the grounding force for me, and I think it's because it feels the least intimidating. Because if you're thinking to yourself, *I'm sitting down and I'm going to write a whole poem*, or not only that, but, *I'm going to write a masterful poem*, the entire idea can just overwhelm you completely. I'm often reminded of this wonderful book that I don't think was given enough credit, Carolyn Forché's *The Blue Hour*, in which she writes a long poem beginning with each of the letters from A to Z. I think of her practice as meditative. She listed the simplest and yet most profound images. I often find that's the way I naturally begin. I lay down one image and then another. Layer upon layer, so that it begins to build itself naturally. If I begin this way I don't become overwhelmed by the moment I'm trying to reach, or the epiphany I'm trying to get to, or even the overarching questions that I'm asking, because all of that can seem too much for me. But if I just remind myself to create those images one after another, then I think I'll get to the place I need to be. I have faith. Faith that I'll reach that moment of revelation. Maybe it's a little bit different for you?

TRACY K. SMITH

Well, I feel like that belief in the image really speaks directly to Eliot, too, and the idea of the objective correlative. The emotional and subjective experience can best be conveyed by way of some external marker or an image, so instead of saying, *I am sad*, look at the world through the lens of that feeling, and what you see is going to bear the traces of that. I feel like that's part of the DNA of a poem, and the way that those particular feelings are laid up against the world so that they color what is seen and how it is seen. I think it is part of every successful poem. That's one of the ways in which Eliot was pretty brilliant.

9

A. M. Homes & Leigh Newman

A. M. HOMES

Leigh, when did you first have a sense that your family was different?

LEIGH NEWMAN

About three years ago, when I decided to write a memoir. I think we all grow up with this notion that the way we grow up is the way other people grow up.

A.M. HOMES

Not me.

LEIGH NEWMAN

Maybe that's better. I think embracing your difference is the way to go. But I come from people who don't talk. In Alaska, they talk about fish or about caribou. So I never really talked about my past much.

A. M. HOMES

Did you have a sense of looming danger or insecurity? Your father was this hyper-competent person, but it also seems like there was an undercurrent of fear that it could all go terribly wrong at any given second.

LEIGH NEWMAN

That's correct. I think denial is one of those ever-reliable emotions, and I grew up with it. Even though I knew that danger was always around the corner—and clearly through the book I almost died like eight hundred times—I always thought my dad would fix it. So I wasn't as scared as I should have been. It was a combination of your youthful understanding that you're not going to die because you're young—and also thinking your dad is a hundred feet tall in hip boots.

A. M. HOMES

Can you talk about the decision to write a memoir? What finally prompted you to write the book?

LEIGH NEWMAN

Total abject failure. I wrote a novel, and it didn't work. I think it was well written, but it just flopped as a story. It had too many narrators. When you fail at something you have to think about what you did, and change it radically. So I had written a novel about Alaska, about a bunch of swashbucklers who lived in Anchorage with a lot of money and guns and power and shopping malls. I had also written an essay in *Tin House*, a funny essay about food and chicken-frying caribou. I thought I had to do something, or I might actually go into a tailspin. So I'd better do something completely different—

something I don't even want to do, but something I think I might be able to do.

A. M. HOMES

What was that process like? I know in terms of myself that writing *The Mistress's Daughter* was like picking at a wound, or picking at a scab every day thinking, "Let's see if I can get it to bleed again today," as though that was fun. Was it a kind of excavation, did you learn things that you didn't think that you had remembered?

LEIGH NEWMAN

I actually felt in many ways it was a relief. I'd been writing and looking at the videotape for so long, it had interfered with my life in so many ways. There was no point or place that I went in the world where I wasn't thinking about these things. I just wasn't talking about them, ever. So writing about it was deeply personal and deeply emotional. I would often kind of fall apart. I don't think it was a fun time to be around me. I felt like I had to gallop through it, like I was ice-skating on this very, very thin ice, and underneath the ice was every single person and every single thing that ever happened to me, sort of yelling at me. I had to keep going or I was going to fall through. So I would really gallop through the pages, and then cry, and then go do something stupid like go eat a big meatball sub. There was this Chinese restaurant with fried chicken and I would go there every day and ask for six pieces of fried chicken and a Coke.

A. M. HOMES

Is there a sense of relief now?

LEIGH NEWMAN

I feel a sense of ownership.

A. M. HOMES

Of yourself?

LEIGH NEWMAN

Yes, and I wasn't expecting it. I went into it just trying to write a good story. I had been trying to write something hard and compelling and true and language-focused and that's what I went in for. But, again, denial, my friend, we walked through three hundred pages together. At the end I realized that the book did change my life. It gave me confidence. I also wrote the memoir out of love for my parents. Things were really radical and eccentric in my house. People were almost dying all of the time, and fighting, and burning down houses. But I loved my parents, and it was a great way of looking at them and finding an adult sense of love for them: where you understand all their flaws and why things went wrong, but you love them all the same.

A. M. HOMES

In your daily work as an editor you are working constantly with writers. What was your experience as a writer and how has that changed your work?

LEIGH NEWMAN

I wrote the book kind of loose-cannonish for the first two years. Then the last year I was editing other people and I learned a lot. With nonfiction you really have to make friends with telling a little bit more than with fiction. That is something, a skill. So I've been working with all of these wonderful writers: Jim Shepard and Jeffrey Eugenides, and last week, Toni Morrison. You really do see the value of telling, and how to use it to your best advantage in nonfiction.

A. M. HOMES

How about your relationship to fact and to accuracy? Often, as a novelist, when I'm writing nonfiction I'm very aware of what is fact and what is not.

LEIGH NEWMAN

It was a disaster. I was calling up my dad, for the first year, every five minutes. I'd be like, "Was it Grove Peak or Rainbow Peak? What kind of plane were we in?" I called up the Alaska State Library and made friends with the librarian. She's mentioned in the credits. Actually, in the book at one point it says there's an eight-point-six earthquake, the Great Alaskan Earthquake, but that was the number I got from what hit in Anchorage. Elsewhere in Alaska it was nine-point-two. So many people read the book and they want to dispute me on that.

A. M. HOMES

Those fact-checkers, you got to be careful.

LEIGH NEWMAN

Yes, daggers, daggers in the eyes. So those are the fact parts, and then the question is what actually happened.

A. M. HOMES

What about the emotional parts? The emotional truth of things?

LEIGH NEWMAN

I gave the book to both of my parents.

A. M. HOMES

How did that go?

LEIGH NEWMAN

It went okay. I think everybody was shocked. They had this idea that I was writing a book about fishing and hunting. I also had this idea. This was the worst part. My parents were totally supportive while I was writing. I gave them the book expecting them to be like, "Yeah! Great job, honey." My dad was like, "Oh, my God." We cut out a couple of things together that were emotionally untrue. He is actually a very good reader. A big outdoorsman, who also plays classical piano, huge reader, kind of sophisticated in his tastes, and he cut out maybe three scenes, but they were good cuts. I'd dissolved into that judgy tone, which I so did not want to be in the memoir.

A. M. HOMES

What did it sound like?

LEIGH NEWMAN

Whining. The Great Alaskan anti-quality. They were a little whiny.

A. M. HOMES

Whining in Alaska only refers to an engine. It's never used for a human, is it? I don't think humans whine in Alaska.

LEIGH NEWMAN

They don't. They go under the water or they stay up and talk.

A. M. HOMES

Are there things about Alaskan cuisine that we would want to know?

LEIGH NEWMAN

Honestly, yes. When I first came to New York I never ate any salmon and was a total snob. It wasn't real salmon, but like poached Atlantic mess. It's a hot mess, very different from Pacific salmon, especially wild fresh Pacific salmon. But now you can just order all the salmon you want. They catch it in the water, they freeze it on the boats, they ship it out. It seriously is as good as you're going to get in Alaska. It's like email, they're emailing the salmon to us.

A. M. HOMES

Have you ever killed and eaten anything on your own there?

LEIGH NEWMAN

A lot of ducks. I was big into shooting ducks as a kid. I could shoot them but I just couldn't hit them. I'd go out hunting and I'd be shooting holes at the sky. I'm a little blind, I'm out of practice, the ducks run away. There always is a catch in my throat, though. I think it might be psychosomatic. I like watching wild things be free. That is what stopped me from killing. There's a scene in the book where I talk about trying to kill a caribou, which is a big tradition in Alaska. You go out with your dad, you kill it and butcher it. I refused to do it when I was thirteen.

A. M. HOMES

We have that here, it's called a bar mitzvah. Though the rituals are slightly different. But, what happened? You went out with him?

LEIGH NEWMAN

I went out and I refused to do it and I brought a camera with me. I somehow pretended that I was going to make a photo essay. He thought I was going to take pictures of him killing this caribou, and that he would look like a butcher. And that I would keep them, and make him look like a bad guy. I know he was thinking this, and in fact I was also thinking this. But once again, no access to the narrative in your brain. We tromped through the woods . . . Actually, there are really no woods in Alaska, it's really just miles and miles of empty tundra and it's very spongy.

A. M. HOMES

Spongy Alaska. We haven't seen those books on "Spongy Alaska" yet. Is it squishy?

LEIGH NEWMAN

It's squishy. You squish along and half of them are sinkholes that you fall into. And when you're carrying a gun, a pack, chest waders, you can really sink under and it's hard to get out. We would just hike for seven or eight miles and then just camp on the ground. My dad was a big fan of not bringing enough gear, and so often it would be like, okay, let's just lie down in the dirt and sleep. Now he's gotten older and he likes canned food.

A. M. HOMES

Do you have a firearm in New York? Do you feel safe?

LEIGH NEWMAN

I don't have a firearm, absolutely not. I'm pro–gun control, and I feel like a gun in a city environment is just you waiting to shoot your neighbor because they came in to borrow a candle in the middle of the night.

A. M. HOMES

And in Alaska is that any different?

LEIGH NEWMAN

No, it's not actually any different. I grew up in a house like that. We had a very clear gun closet that was built into the bottom of the house, so if anyone broke into my house my father would have had to go down two stories of stairs, go out, then take the ammo out of the ammo drawer, put it into the gun, load it. It would have to have been the slowest criminal in the world.

Questions from the Audience

How did your experiences growing up affect your child-rearing today?

LEIGH NEWMAN

I think on the one hand they made me much more on it as a parent. I'm like the classic New York parent: you must go to school, get out of bed. I skipped a lot of school. On the other hand, I'm more adamant about teaching responsibility to kids. Even just simple things, like, "You want a glass of water? Go get it." My little one is three. I want him to be able to put on his own clothes, get his own water, brush his own teeth. I've taught them how to ski, I've taught them how to fish. I've taken them on duck-hunting trips with me in Idaho. I do want them to have that exposure to the wild in a way that impresses on your imagination.

A. M. HOMES

I was curious about the sense of being an outsider wherever you were, and this is both as a writer and also in thinking about Alaska. How did you manage to write about that?

LEIGH NEWMAN

One of the things I most related to with your memoir, and I thought a lot about, was the sense of illegitimacy. My parents divorced, my father stayed in Alaska, he remarried, and he had two kids. I was living with my mom in Baltimore, and we didn't have a lot of money and things were very tough and my mom was up and down. Then I would come back and see my dad and everything there would be the perfect Alaskan life. You know, they'd have cross-country skis with wax. They'd have Patagonia pullovers, matching. And the kids were going to the school that I would have gone to if I'd lived there. For me that was excruciating, I'm not going to lie. That was a real sense of loss and I never talked about it. I never wanted my brothers to feel the things that I had felt. I was so afraid of talking about it with my dad. I felt like he had chosen his second wife over me, and my mom, and if I made a big problem he was going to do it again. I think that's the bass note of that situation. I guess there are bolder kids who tell their parents, but my dad was a god with a fly rod and I couldn't do it, I couldn't make the words come to my mouth. It took me a long time to get over it.

So you've talked about the denial that you've lived in with your family. Now that you've written the book, has it changed?

LEIGH NEWMAN

No, my parents are completely behind the book. They've both called me and been like, "I support you, I'm really excited about the book." But we never discuss it. My two younger brothers have both come out and written me beautiful letters and they've been very supportive in all of the events. My mom went to a reading in Baltimore. Look, denial is always given this bad rap. Just like fear is given a bad rap, just like competency is always given a good rap. There are always multiple sides to these things. Quite frankly, we all know how to function. I said what I needed to say. Everybody knows it. Everybody has dealt with it. We had beautiful long conversations when they were reading the manuscript. Life-changing, intimate conversations. Now I feel like everyone thinks we've all said enough.

10

Wendy Lesser & Robert Pinsky

WENDY LESSER

I was thinking there are really two notions of the poetic role. A much older one, from the Homeric through Renaissance at least and beyond that into the eighteenth century, of the poet as public figure expressing public concerns, for the most part, of representing public people in some way, or describing public people. Then there's the Romantic notion, which carries through heavily to our time, of the private, the personal, and everything coming out of the interior of the poet's life. Normally these are seen as two conflicting parts, or roles, for the poet, but they seem to be blended in your work. I wanted to ask you if you could comment on this blending. In your life, is there a conflict between the public poet, the Poet Laureate, the person who has to do the public poems and be out there on television, and the man who has to sit in the room and write the poems?

ROBERT PINSKY

I was not a successful teenager. I was not the kind of kid who would be elected class president or go to Harvard. I was put into the Dumb Class in the eighth grade and I graduated from high school in the lower third of my class. Playing music probably kept me from falling apart completely. So I have a bit of the failure's scorn for official, public things like Poet Laureate. On that old level, it's all kind of stupid to me: titles, prizes, Professor, Ph.D. . . . I have the failure's defensive skepticism and scorn towards such things that are officially designated as important. I don't think Harvard is more important than a community college. I don't take Poet Laureate as—

WENDY LESSER

Harvard is less public than a community college.

ROBERT PINSKY

Yes. Certainly schools of that category are less important to our society than community colleges.

Now, on the other hand, I'm very proud of the Favorite Poem Project, with the videos at favoritepoem.org, and I do understand that it was enabled by the title Poet Laureate. Furthermore, I've raised a family, I have children and grandchildren. I appreciate what a nice life I have, and I know that this partly involves acquiescence to certain basic worldly patterns . . . patterns that I guess turn out to be more forgiving as you get older, if you're a certain kind of person.

When Rilke talks about angels—and whether we'll hear them or not—he may seem to epitomize one of the kinds of poet you're talking about, the inwardness of German Romanticism. But Rilke acknowledges that he is a product of history all the time. He makes a point about this in his language, as much as Paul Celan, who also acknowledges history, in a quite different way. It was impossible for Paul Celan not to write about the Holocaust, where his parents perished—and in writing in one of the many languages he knew growing up. German was the language of culture and art. Celan was compelled to write in it, though he tried to do that in a way that made German itself writhe, to reflect his own agony, so the language seems to be coming apart.

The public/interior distinction—if we look at the poets we admire the most and elevate, like Dante, well, he embodies breaking down of that distinction. In his greatest work, Dante's cosmology is tied up with, and responds to, his personal grudges. In the first third of *The Inferno* he spends energy trying to stop himself from being so angry at the football coach in the tenth grade. And he's still trying to get back at him, though he knows it's idiotic that he doesn't get beyond it. The personal, you know, it's all got to do with a crush on an unattainable girl. And Dante's classical learning, Christian learning, cosmology, politics, it's all tied up completely with who he is in particular. The girl, the coach. He also knows he's a product of history. All of us here have histories, and we didn't invent those.

WENDY LESSER

Now, the good thing about the passing of time since a work was written is that we don't need to know who that football coach was. In other words, you can read the Dante passages without knowing the source of the particular grudge, and just feel the strength of it and the anger.

ROBERT PINSKY

Yes! He's such a good writer that you know exactly what it is and understand, although we have footnotes and an immense amount of scholarship. That's useful. We're glad it's there. But I agree, the way he writes it you don't have to know a lot about Branca d'Oria. He says, wait a second, Branca's not dead, I've seen him: he wears pants and eats. And the devil explains, well, some souls are so corrupt and evil that they come down here before they die—a devil is driving Branca's body around, in the world above.

WENDY LESSER

Since you raised Dante, I'd like to ask you about your work as a translator. You did these very good translations of Dante and Milosz and some of the Hebrew poets you've decided to write through or with, but what does it do for you to take on their voices or language?

ROBERT PINSKY

I'm not sure I know the answer. To an extent, it just eases one of the difficult parts of writing, which is knowing what to say next. And translation, the way I do it, is exactly like writing a poem. There is no difference. It is the same imagination process, and the same kind of verbal, audible process . . . except you don't have to think about what to say next. In some ways translation's just a relatively easy way to be writing poetry.

But that's a little superficial, because (among other things) translation is also the best form of reading. Just think about those people in the Renaissance, like Sir Philip Sidney and his sister Mary. Literary theory; creative writing; history of literature—all of these things were learned by translation. The little schoolkids, I guess they'd get up and do prayers before dawn and then they'd translate Greek hexameters into Latin elegiac couplets. The whole education was based on translation and they grew up to love learning. (Despite the brutality, in a way, of the learning process.) And they produced great literature. So translation—what does it do for one?—it is the highest form of study.

WENDY LESSER

I was looking at your book *Selected Poems*, and realized it's organized in reverse chronological order. Why? Normal selection goes from oldest to newest.

ROBERT PINSKY

When I started publishing my poetry I felt I was going very much against the prevailing grain, and part of that was writing long poems. *An Explanation of America*, my second book, is a book-length poem. *Sadness and Happiness*, my first book, contains the quite long title poem. Also, at the end of *Sadness and Happiness* there's another long poem called "Essay on Psychiatrists." Those titles—"an explanation of"; the two common abstractions of "sadness and happiness" and "essay on" psychiatrists—were expressing something rebellious, but also something in me. I wanted to feel free to talk. And to talk not as "the speaker," but as Robert Pinsky. The name on the front cover of the book, that's who was saying the poems.

So: I don't go back on that, but with *Selected Poems* I thought about people who might be new to my work, someone who might be eighteen or twenty-one or twenty-four years old, maybe just picking it up in a bookstore. I don't want to say to that person, "You now must read a very long poem," or necessarily excerpt those early, expansive poems. So the reverse chronological order was a practical matter: a way to have poems that looked rather like poems early on in the book. It's poetry, so I want it to look like what a new reader might think poetry would look like. Then the first poem of the book is called "Rhyme." A favorable reviewer said, "It's just like Robert Pinsky to write a poem called 'Rhyme' that does not rhyme." But, in fact, it does, in its way.

WENDY LESSER

When you published your earliest book you were married to an English teacher, and now to a psychoanalyst. They are the same person, but still . . .

ROBERT PINSKY

Yes, Wendy—we hasten to say it's the same woman!

WENDY LESSER

I was wondering if this transformation was in any way reflected in your poetry. Then in *Selected Poems* I found that last poem—which chronologically is really the first—"Essay on Psychiatrists." There's a lot of what one might call Freudian digging in those early poems.

ROBERT PINSKY

The present Mrs. Pinsky—*Doctor* Pinsky—to whom I have been married for fifty years, was just driven to become a mental health professional . . . [*laughter*] She is a very good reader and is still one of the three or four people I depend upon to read drafts of my poems.

She was an English teacher in the eighth/ninth grade of independent schools, and then started a new intellectual endeavor, based on reading she'd been doing for years. I think that did give me new ideas that were coming into my life, by listening to her conversation.

WENDY LESSER

Who is really worth reading among poets and prose writers? Let's limit it to those among the dead.

ROBERT PINSKY

Good! An ambitious writer who simply reads his/her contemporaries and his/her teacher's generation is failing to get a leg up. You're falling back. If you want to do something great, find those who the super-talented aren't reading. It's important to read things you think are magnificent and that are very remote—other languages far from you, as well as distant in time—but I shouldn't choose the reading for you. You should feel compelled to look around and find things for yourself. William Butler Yeats says there's no singing school but studying monuments of singing's magnificence. The young poet should find things to read the way an ambitious musician listens to things, or an ambitious actor watches plays and films. It should be something you think is monumentally magnificent and it shouldn't be something that Wendy Lesser or Robert Pinsky chooses. *You* must choose, and Yeats doesn't say "be familiar with" or "look at." He says "*studying* monuments of its own magnificence."

I give this assignment to anyone who takes a poetry course with me, writing or reading: They have to type up an anthology of things that they think are magnificent. Examples that they would stand behind. You know, when you type something you're memorizing it three words at a time. So if nothing else, you're reading something you admire slowly. And you're being forced to choose, and choosing, like the physical typing and memorizing, is . . . *good for you*. It's nutritious! (And it tastes good.)

WENDY LESSER

You talked about your wife being one of your good readers, and I also know that you have a circle that includes Louise Glück and Frank Bidart and maybe others. Can you talk a little bit about what it's like to write poetry in that situation, where you come up with something and then other people give you their two cents' worth, or maybe more than two cents' worth?

ROBERT PINSKY

It's a traditional thing among poets. If anyone here knows both fiction writers and poets . . . Fiction is an industrial revolution product. Picture those pages, perfectly symmetrical rectangles. A certain kind of machine produces that rectangle and binds it. When we reproduce it electronically we still have a justified right and left margin, to market. Poetry is older and more aristocratic, so that the circle of Philip Sidney and his sister, the Countess of Pembroke, and their poet friends like Fulke Greville, they gathered at leisure and talked about one another's verses and conferred about them. They didn't make a big distinction between translation and composition. Originality was not in your ideas, but in your style. So whether you were imitating a poem, or translating, or you felt free to combine translating with adapting, changing it a bit—that was not a big distinction for them. That also was aristocratic—nobody was doing anything as vulgar as *publishing* their work, selling it. The idea was, you were simply doing something beautiful. So I'm not cheating Catullus or Statius. If I take Statius's poem on sleep and it's a fifteen-line poem and I turn it into a sonnet, it's just amusing to me to do it and I'll show it to my friends and see if they're amused by it. It's not middle-class *property*.

Now, fiction writers are different from that. They tend to say, "I'll show it to you when it's finished." It's "mine"—property. It's, "I'll show *my* novel to *my* agent so he can pitch it for selling to *my* publisher." Poets are more likely to say, "What do you think of this? I'm working on it." For fiction writers, it tends to be less sociable, more proprietary. That, too, to go back to our first topic—that, too, has a history.

We all have emails now. I live near Frank and Louise, but I don't live near Charlie Williams, and so I can email him a draft of my poem, continuing poetry's long history of being somewhat social and collaborative in a way that other forms of composition may not be. As with ancient Chinese poets. Poets are not like the characters in Balzac's *Lost Illusions*. In that novel, the two main characters are the young poet Lucien and his friend, whose name I forget, who is literally in the paper business. They both are, and Lucien as I remember abandons poetry and becomes a journalist.

Speaking of great novels about writers in middle-class settings, I'd like to add that I think everyone here should read *Ulysses*. You don't have to read it straight through: just read it dipping in here and there, like a book of poems. And everyone should own a copy of the John Williams anthology of Renaissance poetry. And read William Carlos Williams's *In the American Grain*.

WENDY LESSER

It's so perverse of you to answer my last question, instead of this one.

ROBERT PINSKY

That's me all over.

Questions from the Audience

What would you like to translate next, if anything?

ROBERT PINSKY

I don't know. I never planned to do *The Inferno.* Somebody suggested it to me and then I got going on it. I don't know if I ever will translate again. There was a time people in my category in high school were not allowed to take the high-class language, French, so we were confined to take the language of Cervantes: we took Spanish. There was a time when I was not bad in Spanish, so if it were translating anything, then I'd probably look around in language I used to know a little bit. I knew Spanish in a way that I'm not so hot in Italian or Hebrew or Polish. If I were going to guess, the next thing would be Spanish, where I can actually at least fake it if you hum a few bars for me.

What role does music play in your work?

ROBERT PINSKY

Music informs my writing entirely. It's what I spend most of my energy on. I think about music the most, and it really goes back to early childhood. I remember as a child, maybe even in my crib, I was tapping out the rhythm of sentences on the headboard. And thinking about the melody of sentences as well, the pitches. Every sentence has its melody.

In those difficult years of high school I was the music man. I was maybe afraid of trying to do something verbal. I don't know what the problem was, with school, but there was a problem. And yet I was always sort of a good talker. And I read a lot. Music was less my natural gift, but my band was the one

that played the school's rock and roll dances. In the popularity poll, I was voted Most Musical Boy.

Pianist Lawrence Hobgood and I recently made our second "PoemJazz" CD, *House Hour.* I read my poems and try to use the sentences as melodic phrases, in conversation with Laurence's beautiful, inventive playing.

WENDY LESSER

Your reference to your crib made me remember that in one of your poems, you describe climbing down out of your crib and going into your parents' room. Do you actually remember being in your crib?

ROBERT PINSKY

Nobody is going to believe me, but yes, I do.

WENDY LESSER

How long did they keep you there?

ROBERT PINSKY

I was twenty-eight.

WENDY LESSER

Robert Duncan used to say he could remember being months old, but I didn't ever believe him.

ROBERT PINSKY

I don't know how old you are when you get out of you for the first time, but I woke up and figured out a v climb out, almost falling out, and I went into their be where they were still sleeping. It must have been a wee can remember them laughing, it was all very nice, an

this is all very Freudian—they picked me up and put me in the bed. We were all three of us laughing. I climbed out by myself and it was, "*Look at that!*" A moment of tremendous happiness. Did I make it up? I don't think so, but I can't prove it to you.

I wanted to hear your thoughts about the literary canon.

ROBERT PINSKY

I don't believe in "the" canon, like an academic's list. Excellence is real, and the body of it is always evolving, always changing. The important thing is to find something you love. Each reader. Also, each teacher. My answer, if a teacher asks, "What should I teach?": something you love. Kids can smell it, if you don't really like something "canonical" but you're trying to pretend you do. It doesn't matter how arcane or difficult a work is—if you love it, share it. You might think, "Oh, it's a class of boys, so let's find a poem about sports." No. If what touches you is a poem about death, you should read that to the boys. And expect them to respect it, as you respect them by giving it to them.

What would you say to the young poet, in terms of how they should structure their lives?

ROBERT PINSKY

My advice: read a lot, notice a lot. Read what?—everybody is different, so as with the canon, I don't like making prescriptions. Ezra Pound recommends translation for young poets, because it keeps the subject from wobbling around: you have to stick to the original subject.

One is distracted by many things as a teenager—almost

as many as at my age. I think that all of us crave something difficult: that's why video games are so popular. And that's why people who become very successful in this country—we likely find them walking through the greensward with little sticks pushing a little white ball around. As an animal we crave difficulty—even more than pleasure, I think. Contrary to the travel industry, what we really want most is a nice juicy difficulty to engage—to engage, not even to solve, necessarily. For a long time in my life, music was the best difficulty I had. It was infinitely difficult. No one ever is perfect at it. The greatest players practice, and it's objective in a certain way: whether you're keeping time or not, your intonation is there or not. It resembles the difficulties of a game, but it's more subtle and has more to do with feeling. Poetry, the same. What one hopes to provide for children, for the young, is a worthy difficulty. Difficulties they can relish, and that will also be productive for the rest of us. Easier said than done. And competence: difficulty and its reflection, competence.

WENDY LESSER

Along the lines of that question, somebody once said to me as a writer, beware of your strengths. I found that useful advice, actually. I wondered if you agree with that.

ROBERT PINSKY

My first response to "beware of your strengths" is, yes—don't be complacent in what you can do. Mastery is . . . I'm wondering how much to plagiarize the essay I haven't written, that I have to write about poetry, and I was thinking about forms of deprecation. You master something and unless you're stretching to make yourself get better you start using your settled mastery to deprecate things. In poetry I can think of two extremes of that. At one extreme the genteel, jovial, amusing chum, smirking: "*I know that nothing is very serious or important.*" That tone. And the opposite is surprisingly similar, is equally glib or knowing, as well as "experimental": "*I know language can't do anything, language is completely useless and incompetent, it's illusory, it's just a closed system.*" In contrast, if I think about the high modernists who inspired me when I was a kid—you know, *A Portrait of the Artist as a Young Man*, Yeats's late poetry, Cather, Faulkner, Williams. The aspiration. It's the opposite of deprecation. It's daringly grand, very large. When I think about "beware of what you're good at" I think of urgent aspiration—feeling yourself get further, struggling with something you haven't done yet . . . because the reality, the subject matter, is important.

11

Renata Adler & David Shields

with Lucas Wittmann

LUCAS WITTMANN

Thank you all for joining us. I am absolutely thrilled to be up here with two writers that I admire, though I can assure you that I'm not as excited as the two of them are to be up here together, as I learned backstage. They're each other's greatest fans, I think. So, let's get right into it. Renata, it must be very exciting to find your books being reissued thirty years later, and to be getting such wonderful praise. Can you tell us a little bit about how it feels?

RENATA ADLER

Well, it's very peculiar; it's like being this sort of found fossil. It just feels very strange. Here I am, and they'd been out of print for a very long time, and then David, it's just . . . I don't know if they still have the Hollywood legend of being found at Schwab's Pharmacy, but here I am, this fossil found at Schwab's drugstore by David and by other people who said, well, why doesn't somebody reprint it? And then for the longest time, nobody did. I mean, they said it in 2010. It was this body that said, "We'd like to have this reprinted," and then nothing happened, and now it's been reprinted. So it's very odd. They still look familiar, I must say.

LUCAS WITTMANN

David, you started the call for Renata's books to be brought back into print, and you've read *Speedboat* two dozen times?

DAVID SHIELDS

I've been teaching the book for many, many years over and over again and I just sort of selfishly wanted the book back in print so I didn't have to surreptitiously teach it. It's just a real consummation for me to be here, to be with Renata Adler. She really changed my writing life—I would say in many ways really saved my writing life, and she changed the trajectory of my work completely. I was at an impasse with my work and I read and reread her book *Speedboat* and *Pitch Dark* over and over again, and I watched the Ross McElwee film *Sherman's March* over and over again, and those works completely changed my writing life. So the idea that I had something to do indirectly with the books of Renata's being reprinted—I could pretty much die and go to heaven. My work has been done.

LUCAS WITTMANN

How did they change your writing?

DAVID SHIELDS

I had written one very traditional novel—my first novel—published almost thirty years ago. I wrote a second novel, a bildungsroman, a growing-up novel, that was somewhat more formally playful, but still relatively hamstrung by narrative, and then I was starting to play around in a third book, novels and stories, called *A Handbook for Drowning*, that mixed between the essay and story. A little bit of collage, but a lot of relatively formally straitjacketed stories as well. Then I was trying to write what I thought was my fourth book, a book called *Remote*, trying to write that as a novel. For a number of reasons, I could not get the novelistic machinery to operate with that book. I found myself sort of incapable of developing those things that are apparently quite crucial to novels, like settings and plots and characters. And so I was endlessly reading and rereading *Speedboat* and *Pitch Dark* and I absolutely loved those works' compression, precision, the way they let a thousand discrepancies bloom at once, the way they tell multiple stories simultaneously, and above all the way, as in Proust, narrative is being used as a vector on a larger philosophical grid. Stories aren't being told just to tell stories but those narrative vectors that Renata unleashed in *Pitch Dark* and *Speedboat* are part of a much richer philosophical meditation that is full of enormous questions for me. That thrilled me to my toes, and still thrills me to my toes.

LUCAS WITTMANN

Renata, we know how David arrived at his books by reading yours, but when you read his books did you find yourself—the shock of recognition, that here was someone who understood—

RENATA ADLER

Well, that's the funny thing, it only occurred to me recently. Here we are, we think all of the time, we have our consciousness, the stuff we pay attention to, don't pay attention to, things change. Just the last few days, I thought of something. I don't know how many of you write, and I don't know how this is for David, but I think this is true. When I was writing, it turns out—what was I doing? I was addressing a situation. When you write, you address a situation. You don't realize that. You realize it in nonfiction, because you're addressed or reporting something. You try to report it as accurately as you can, that's nonfiction. If you're writing an essay, you are addressing a situation because you maybe want to persuade people. It may just be that you feel you must write, that nature intended you to be a writer, or you think you can make money at it, or anything. You want to be famous, whatever sorts of reasons people write for. But the situation is interior. It's not wanting someone to realize that something is a complete fraud. So starting out writing nonfiction, but then thinking all writers write fiction, and when I was thinking about it I realized the only work that mattered to me was fiction. When you're addressing plot, which preoccupies both of us in much the same way, it occurred to me it's sort of a mixed thing about real life. People saying, is this autobiographical, is this fiction, is it real. I think that's just in a way a crazy question because what you're doing the minute you say, "This is fiction," is you've changed the game completely. I realized from your book that that's had more of an impact on me than real life, and so this division is in a way fake because I care more—I mean, I wish that Juliet would not commit suicide, and I wish it every time that I'm reading about a plot, and I care more, in a way . . .

Okay, let me go back in this crazy way to something else. There was a time in Hollywood when the story became no longer the story on the screen, of the plot on the screen, but the actors. There was this time when the actors became the plot. Everyone was making up fantasy lives for these actors, and there were magazines like *Modern Screen*, and there was suddenly an offscreen plot, which were the lives of these actors. Then there came the moment, which was a wonderful moment, of the auteur theory. So, the director became a character for everybody. And then a truly horrible moment when the critique—when suddenly on billboards you saw what some damn critique had to say, as if that mattered in the slightest. But, okay, so who is in the plot?

So then there's the plot in one's own life, where one wishes certain things to happen. And the people that one loves, one wishes certain things to happen for them. There are these wishes that one has of how it's going to go, and that's sort of indispensable in plot, one would think. But, well, first of all I thought, what does one wish in *Hamlet*? One doesn't wish—well, I wish you'd go off and kill your father. Or I wish you'd be nicer to Ophelia. I mean, we have no position in this, but with a thriller it's just very this kind of body-wish that one has, one wants to go this way and not that way, and yet reading the same thing knowing it's going to end badly, and yet still wishing it would go another way. Why can't we do that in fiction? And I think we can, actually, but the rule has changed in a funny way. What you don't especially want is the reader on the writer's side to such an extent, or even aware of the writer to such an extent, that the whole experience of reading fiction is gone. You want the reader not to worry about this performance. So there's a kind of criticism that says—look, I know just what she's up to. You don't want that. What you don't want is for someone to say, oh, look, there's a very interesting technique, and identify with the writer, because that's not the experience of reading fiction. But somehow the writer became the main character in the fiction, and that's the predicament we're stuck in and try to address as narrators. Does that not . . . ?

DAVID SHIELDS

No, that rings true. I have all kinds of things I can say, but Lucas, did you want to jump in?

RENATA ADLER

I didn't mean to go on for so long.

DAVID SHIELDS

I think that was such a Renata moment for me, where there were ninety-seven digressions that ended with this absolutely crucial epiphany, which is the fourth law of thermodynamics: the perceiver by his very presence alters what he perceives—it is the key postmodern philosophical moment, and I think a lot of Renata's work, and I hope in a different key my own work, proceeds from that realization. I also admire in Renata's work, in *Speedboat* and *Pitch Dark* in particular, the way in which the private and the public come together, the ways in which fiction and nonfiction are conflated, stand-up comedy and political polemics stand side by side. I think a lot of what Renata was talking about has to do with, to my ear, a weariness with the authoritarian narrator. So much of what is astonishing about *Pitch Dark* and *Speedboat* has to do with the ways in which Renata Adler got to, for an American audience, earlier than most American writers, these sort of poststructuralist ideas about the ways in which language and communication change everything. Virtually everything about the book, say, *Speedboat*, has to do with the warping nature of communication. The epigraph, if you remember—we were talking about it backstage and Renata said, "I just sort of threw in the epigraph at the end, I'm not sure why," and I hope that was false humility, because the entire book builds off the epigraph, where it reads, "'What war?' said the Prime Minister sharply. 'No one has said anything to me about a war. I really think I should have been told.' And presently, like a circling typhoon the sounds of the battle begin to return." This is from Evelyn Waugh's *Vile Bodies.* To me so much of the book is in that epigraph. The ways in which language doesn't just register life, it absolutely creates it and prophesies it, and specifically the ways in which language creates in its miscommunication psychic and cultural and even political violence. Human beings can never totally understand one another, and out of that frustration comes cultural cataclysm, and so much of that, to me, is encrypted to me in that epigraph. It's so much of what *Speedboat* is about.

RENATA ADLER

Well, I didn't mean, David, that it was by accident. It's just that I so loved it I wanted it in there somewhere. I just loved it. *Vile Bodies* is so wonderful and so good. Well, I'm from Newtown, Connecticut, right, that's where I live. So I thought, do I write about this or not, and I thought probably not because it's sort of exploiting what's there, but I probably will. But a funny, strange thing happened to me about literature and its impact on one's life. This business of communication and what we have in common, how many generations of it and in what form, and how much of it is literature and how much of it comes from memory, and so, okay. A great gap here, but we use educational law. You're an educator, you use the education you have, you have the memory of your own life in real life, and you have the memory that is imparted to you when you learn. So I thought learning is joining a sort of public memory in a way. Because we're all going to die, and what will be left joins us all as a tribe, or as a species. It's these memories and these languages and these communications that we have in common, including especially literature.

So, here goes. There I am in Newtown. I was reading a lot of classics because I had back trouble. So I was reading *Richard III*, and he's just murdered the children because he wants to be king and he is in fact king. And he says to the mother, "Say they were not slain. Say I slew them not!" And she says, "You slew them not, yet . . ." Now I've forgotten! "Say you slew them not? Then say they are not dead. And dead they are." And that's really powerful when I'm not screwing it up.

Then came the Nuremberg trials, and whoever it was speaking at the Nuremberg trials, speaking of these mass murders. He said toward the end of the trials about these war criminals, "Say you slew them not? Then say they are not dead, but dead they are." He took it and suddenly applied it to six million people. Then in the Neshoba trials, remember three people dead in the Mississippi dam, and John Doar was prosecuting. It was impossible in the South. You could not get a Mississippi jury to convict. And then he said, "Say you slew them not? Then say they are not dead. And dead they are." And there were these three boys dead in the dam. It's a beautiful recurrence, is it not? To me, it's beautiful.

But then, Newtown, and I thought, what do we say? I don't know how you feel about this, but I was going to say these lunatics from the National Rifle Association, and I thought, they say they slew them not—then say they are not slain. Yet dead they are. And there they are, twenty kids in Newtown, and there they are.

Then came this new thing. I don't know if you've noticed, but in the news the last few days they found the bones of Richard III. In a parking lot, right. And before that, this wonderful writer of thrillers, Jospehine Tey, had written a thriller in which she discovered that Richard III did not murder those children, and it's a bum rap through and through. Richard III was perfectly okay. And I thought, gee, reality is as tangled as that. Isn't that pretty tangled? But you couldn't use it in plot, you couldn't use it in an essay, I couldn't even use it tonight. Just for some reason it's on my mind.

[laughter]

DAVID SHIELDS

And yet you did.

RENATA ADLER

And yet I did. Yet dead they are.

LUCAS WITTMANN

I wondered, thinking about Newtown, I wonder if we've lost a bit of that cultural and shared culture. I wonder if you were to say that today, though you did tonight, if one were to say it publicly its resonance would be lost.

RENATA ADLER

That's it. And how much resonance would be lost. And I was wondering about that about memories. At one point I tried to figure out how much, if we didn't remember the worst commercials, the worst songs that everyone knew for no reasons, everything that everyone learned at school, the Mother Goose rhymes, everyone knew these things and in one generation people knew certain things that another generation didn't. I don't know how many of you remember that commercial with a ring around the collar, and it was just for a detergent. Everyone knew that. You can't get rid of it. We've got it, we're stuck with it. But all of those memories we have in common I think will now go. And certain feelings. For example, I was thinking, how much literature will we lose with modern technology? Just take contraception, we wouldn't have *Tess of the D'Urbervilles*, there are all of these predicaments that no longer exist. We just don't have them. One of them—the feeling—you miss somebody and you can't communicate with them because they live two thousand miles away, or they live thirty miles away. There's a feeling for another person that you could have when you couldn't just pick up your cell phone and reach whatever them you're reaching. So there's a whole realm of feeling that is going to be very hard to reach, for any of us.

LUCAS WITTMANN

And yet, speaking of that technological realm—David, you quote from Vonnegut, I think, about how for a modern novelist not to deal with technology is like a Victorian novelist not to deal with sex, or something. But most fiction has missed this changing world of ours, this new technology, this communication.

DAVID SHIELDS

I think a lot of the things I admire about Renata's *Speedboat* and *Pitch Dark* has to do with the ways in which she is fully aware of that, and the ways in which technology plays a major role. In *Speedboat*, for instance, that book, it's called *Speedboat*, after all, and in a lot of ways it's about the ways in which the faster we move, the more violent our emotions become, and the more warped our language becomes, which creates a more thwarted human relationship, which leads to a kind of cyclical violence, so that book is constantly—the emblematic episode of it is of course a moment when a speedboat is going terribly fast on these rocky waves and someone's back breaks, or doesn't quite break.

RENATA ADLER

She keeps bouncing, exuberantly.

DAVID SHIELDS

And there's a conflation in that scene between sexuality and movement and wealth and language and communication, and you realize reading that book over and over again that Adler is trying to teach you what things to look for in a particular scene once you learn what to read for, the book has taught you what it's about. I'm delighted to see *Speedboat* and *Pitch Dark* reissued, and the books are being talked about very positively, as well they should. But there's also a sense that *Pitch Dark* is somehow "about" the quality of being a woman, or *Speedboat* is "about" the 1970s, and I don't read those books as in any way being that journalistic or that topical. I think that *Pitch Dark*, for instance, which has gotten definitely talked about in the reissue, but it's taken me a long time to realize how amazing *Pitch Dark* is. In many ways, *Speedboat* is this unbelievably magical verbal machine, and *Pitch Dark* is this incredible structural machine which is divided into three sections. The first section is to a large degree about the pitch-darkness of a particular relationship—how a couple completely misunderstands each other. The middle section is about a quasi-crime and the misunderstandings between a couple of drivers, and in the third section there's a sense in which the pitch-dark moves from a couple to a crime to society writ large, so as you pull back as though from a painting, the design becomes clear. Renata Adler is trying to show you in *Pitch Dark* how on the micro-level of a relationship, at the middle level of a quasi-public crime, and on a huge cultural level that we are in pitch-dark—that we misunderstand each other in virtually every exchange. I'd love to see that book talked about in this kind of high philosophical level.

And obviously *Speedboat*, too, is drenched in the 1970s, but it also is, as I've tried to push, a very deep meditation on the nature of human communication. Anyway, I'm responding a little bit to Lucas's question about technology. To me Renata Adler was there very early, especially in *Speedboat*. That book is obsessed with velocity, technology. There's an incredible moment with a party line, and the communicatives on the party line think a couple is going to get married, and when the couple realizes that everyone on the party line thinks they're going to get married—they were going to break up—but they get married regardless because everyone on the party line thought they were going to be married. That's this major Adler moment for me. Language creates an event. Language doesn't register events; the language creates the events.

RENATA ADLER

Well, here's something I want to say about David. You take on the whole thing. I mean, you take on simultaneously the questions of the highest abstraction, questions of what is art, and then a manifesto. Always a manifesto. But it struck me that there are these moments when you know exactly what someone is talking about, in real life or in reading. It sounds like a digression, but it's dead-center for me. People said to me, "You have to read *One Hundred Years of Solitude*," and I tried various times. I tried, and I got to page fifty one time, and I got to page one hundred fifty another time, and I thought everyone has the same name and I don't know what this is about, and then one time it just hit. I understood it. I don't know what you think, but I think it's just the most incredible masterpiece. I thought: I get it, where was I before? There's no plot, but the richness of invention. It is so good, and if you haven't read it or failed to read it, try again. When you know what you're talking about, and when other people know what you're talking about, and when I read David I know what he's talking about. A lot of times it happens to me because we only have so much time, and the thing about our lives is really that we die, and that really is so. There are these come-off moments, some of us have them, where all the role-playing that we do just comes off and we really talk about what we mean at that moment. That's a good thing to do. But the final, bottom-line come-off moment is that we'll die, perhaps painfully if no one is watching out for us. And another is quite funny. There are just some people who occasionally say something and they may be ruined, and perhaps unjustly, they don't know what they're talking about, and I won't hear more of that. That's someone I shouldn't be reading, or perhaps I should be more tolerant. No, there are some people who are quite harmful!

You can see I ramble. It's what I do.

DAVID SHIELDS

I wanted to respond. Lucas asked me earlier what have I learned from Renata Adler. A lot of things. The only rule is never be boring. The main thing I learned, among so many things—I can't imagine my writing life without Renata Adler, to be honest—but the main thing I've learned, that I was so envious of for so long, is just how manifestly, blisteringly intelligent she is line by line, page by page, paragraph by paragraph. There's no room to hide. She is just absolutely manifestly intelligent on the page. That's what I realized I wanted to do. I'm smart, too, I want to think. I can be smart on the page. Someone like, say, Raymond Carver. I admire what he does, but it has nothing to do with what I'm interested in. This is our chance. They tell me the thing about life is that one day you'll be dead, and I'm very aware that in fifty years I'll be dead. This is the entire secular ride. And this is our chance to articulate fully the human predicament at this moment. I think a lot of this line of David Foster Wallace, who was asked, "What's so great about writing?" and he said we're existentially alone on the planet. You can't know what I'm thinking and feeling and I can't know what you're thinking and feeling, and writing at its best is a bridge constructed across the abyss of human loneliness. The writing I love, the writing I try to write, the writing I read, the writing I teach, foregrounds strongly the question of how the writer solved the problem of being alive. Samuel Johnson said a book should teach us how to escape existence or to endure existence, and so much of what I love about Renata's work, as well as other people's work that shares those qualities, is that it is manifestly, melodramatically, existentially wrestling with the essential human questions.

RENATA ADLER

Now I remember what my point was about the manifesto. It's this. There is this solitude that we all have. One reads alone and writes alone. At the same time, the world is going on the way it's going. There's a lot of writing about bullying, a lot of gangs out there. Without being paranoid, in a certain way the world falls apart, and in another really just gangs up. What you need is something that brings together people who know what each other are talking about. That's when the boldness of having a manifesto is almost incredible. It's Luther, or it's Marx, except that we're all shy, but there it is, you're starting over. I guess in my way I thought I was starting over, but I didn't mean to. I just wanted to write the kind of novels I like to read. And because I edit a lot I just kept editing, and then I thought where was the part I meant to do, which might have been a thriller or something, and then I thought when I was editing along sooner or later, and then it didn't occur.

LUCAS WITTMANN

Can you explain that a little more? Do you mean that when you were writing it you thought you were writing a thriller?

RENATA ADLER

Yeah, I mean I thought I writing a normal novel. But there came a point where somebody said to me, "You must read Henry James, *The Princess Casamassima*." It's very thick, but I thought, all right, I might read *Princess Casamassima*. And then I got into it. It's brilliant beyond belief. Who has a male hero called Hyacinth? And it's a political novel, it's prescient about radicalism, and it's long. It's a Henry James novel. He must have worked over every word, but he did it in a way I can't do. I just can't do what he does. Those novels seem a kind of miracle to me.

DAVID SHIELDS

Can you talk some more about your composition process? I mean, how did those hundred and seventy pages come together? I'm just kind of selfishly wanting to know.

LUCAS WITTMANN

Especially because everything is so precisely and deliberately, at least it appears to be to the reader, chosen and written.

RENATA ADLER

Well, the only thing in this world I'm compulsively neat about is typing, so the computer is a nightmare for me. I thought it was going to resolve the problem, but it doesn't do anything. I used to type with two fingers and I would make a mistake near the end of the page. Then, no white-out, no eraser, it looked too horrible, so then I had to go back to the beginning of the page, while I'm doing that go back to page one. So it meant a lot of typing of stuff and throwing out of stuff and putting in of stuff and cutting off of stories when this was the whole point I was getting to. That was a surprise to me. At the same time, I thought about plot and suspense when I thought about it at all. I thought you can't do that artificially if I know how this is going to end. So why not do that right at the beginning? Well, you can't, then you have no plot. It's like you can't give the punch line of a joke. Well, I can't tell jokes, either, I thought it's so artificial, so then I thought I'll just see where this goes as a story. Then it turned out for me to be a story about intensity of a certain kind. I don't know what it's a story of. It was by correcting and correcting that I found . . . So now with a computer where you can move everything around at every second and you can have a perfect page, and maybe autocorrect will ruin it for you, but you can have a perfect page, there's almost nothing for me to do. So it doesn't work on computer at all.

LUCAS WITTMANN

Do you write by typewriter, not by hand?

RENATA ADLER

No, I write on the computer, but it's just very confusing. I used to think I wasn't going to lose any work. I used to lose a lot of work because in throwing those pages on the floor and writing notes on checkbooks and wrapping paper, you lose a lot of work that way. But on the computer I forget what I filed it under. It's just a continuous struggle to write on that thing. So, there it is. I just finished what I think is another novel, and I hope this one is more what I was hoping to do with the first one. I do appreciate that you care about *Pitch Dark*, David, because nobody liked it. I mean not nobody, but people certainly didn't like it. And it mattered more to you in ways that I thought were obvious, but it didn't.

DAVID SHIELDS

Why is that?

RENATA ADLER

Well, because this question of modernism and feeling. That is, if you're a certain kind of modernist. Well, let's go to something else. The performing arts. There's no reason to think that a violinist today, anybody in the performing arts, is not as skilled as ever. They practice, and if they play Mozart it's going to affect you in a certain way. Music can affect you. And then there's ballet. So there are the performing arts.

Then there are these arts that I never could find a name for. I kept asking people and they'd say I meant fine art. But what I meant was art that produces an object. So, if you're a sculptor, you have a rock. You do something to the rock and there's something there. You're not performing it, it doesn't depend on your lifetime. You're not doing something that people are meant to watch you doing. You're doing something that will produce a result that's there. A book is like a rock in that sense. So is what a composer writes. It's there, it's a rock. So is a book. So why have they lost the capacity . . . I don't think anybody can do what Dickens could do.

So, I'll get to the point. Soap operas make me cry. Movies make me cry. All that conventional stuff. You can get to those feelings. Dickens makes me cry. But someone writing now like Dickens would be absurd. It'd be great, but it's not what a modernist does. So the modernists I know that sat down to write as modernists had a certain contempt for what I call my housemate syndrome, this sentiment and stuff. What they dread most is kitsch. So there are certain effects they can get. Whimsy. Brilliance. You know what I mean? Regret. It's a certain kind of modernist. I once had a conversation about this. I said, you know, I can't help it, I really like to be moved by what I read. And he said, I hate that. And I know what he meant. There's a kind of corruption that comes with feeling. You know what I mean?

DAVID SHIELDS

In many ways I think your work gave me a way out of all of those issues. You talk about it as though you're kind of exploring it, but *Pitch Dark* and *Speedboat* are the exit maps out of that very conundrum for me.

RENATA ADLER

That's what I want to find for myself!

DAVID SHIELDS

You want to find that sentiment.

RENATA ADLER

Yeah, I want to find my way there, not cheaply.

DAVID SHIELDS

Well, I think those books do. In the prologue to my new book, *How Literature Saved my Life*, I do a long aria to how great Ben Lerner's *Leaving the Atocha Station* is. I don't know if you know that book. Do you like it?

RENATA ADLER

Yes, but because of you!

DAVID SHIELDS

I think what Renata's work represented to me and what Lerner's work represents in a different way is that you have to break out of the sugar factory. There's a men's-commercial, middlebrow, middle-class, bourgeois pressure to pretend that it's not really hard to feel things now. I'm really quite convinced of that. There's a pretense of let's just produce an ordinary narrative, that we feel now the way we used to feel during Balzac's time. It's simply not the case, and if we're honest about it we'll work really hard to create anti-narrative narratives, Adler-like hieroglyphs that move around to create what really it feels like to be alive at ground level now. And that actually moves me immensely. What doesn't move me is false emotion. And Lerner talks about this at length in *Leaving the Atocha Station*, about how what he is moved by is how he goes to a museum and can't be moved by a particular painting. That moves him. That might sound a little too easy or a little too post- post- post-, but that is the condition we're in, I think. I just know it. I know it on my nerve endings. And so do all of you! And the work that really kills, the work that really matters, the work that is doing serious emotional, psychological, philosophical work that is wrestling with that, and for me Renata Adler did that work in a really key way a long time ago. There are plenty of wonderful writers now doing that, whether it's Simon Gray's *The Smoking Diaries*—

RENATA ADLER

He married the sister of an old friend of mine.

DAVID SHIELDS

Really?

RENATA ADLER

That's such a wonderful book.

DAVID SHIELDS

This is the call to arms. Indirectly, I've been pushing Vintage to reissue *The Smoking Diaries*. It's only available in the UK. It is the great book, in my opinion, of the last fifteen years.

LUCAS WITTMANN

I think we have some copies downstairs. I bought some here.

DAVID SHIELDS

It's an incredibly beautiful four-volume book and they published it as a cigarette pack. It's just beautifully done. Incredible book. I swear to god it's a late twentieth century version of Proust or Rembrandt's late self-portraits. There's a whole galaxy of contemporary writers who are following in Renata Adler's footsteps. Leonard Michaels, Simon Gray—

RENATA ADLER

Yeah, but they were all on their way on their own.

DAVID SHIELDS

Of course. But I really like what Renata said about feeling and kitsch and Dickens and soaps. That's the issue for me. The work I really value and that I try to produce is work that tries not to lie about that. That's the work that I find an actual contribution.

LUCAS WITTMANN

Do you go back to Henry James or Dickens, or they don't speak to you anymore? Because, Renata, you still go back?

RENATA ADLER

Not this minute. I did go back to a lot of classics, but not those. So I had this back trouble and I was lying down and I was reading a lot of classical stuff. There was this really amazing thing that happened to me, which is that I realized I hadn't understood, or I'd misremembered some stuff. But that's irrelevant. A lot of stuff where I can't even remember who wrote it. There's this series and someone is the sheriff and I can't remember what they're called, it's not very important, but if there's another one, then I'll read it right away. I'm really anxious to know what happens next. But it's not the same. We are presumably the last of the readers, but it turns out there are more of us than we thought. Isn't that true?

DAVID SHIELDS

I think probably every generation has thought of itself as the last of the readers.

LUCAS WITTMANN

I'm also skeptical of the fact that reading has changed all that much, in a way. I mean, of course there's Twitter and Facebook, but I sometimes think that because it's more transparent, in a way, because there's Kindle and iPad and electronics, that we know more about how people have always been reading. How many times have people tossed aside Dickens or that long piece in a magazine, and we know that now.

RENATA ADLER

I think that's true. Except I remember years ago, Bowden Broadwater, who was married to Mary McCarthy and was a wonderful writer in his own right, and whose secret was what a nice guy he was. He was teaching at St. Barnard's and he said, "No more book reports." And he said, no, you have to stop it, because reading is a pleasure. It's a physical pleasure, and there's something about the motion of the eye and the interaction of everything, and if you have these boys reading with a book report in mind you're already . . . And I thought that's so prescient, because reading on my Kindle, even on my iPad, I just don't know that it's the same reading. I don't know that it's the same act. This happens in every generation. But I do wonder about that blinding computer. I do read on the computer all of the time, but not literature.

LUCAS WITTMANN

I wonder if it's also something to do with memory. It all seems uniform. It's the same white page. Whereas if you have books on the bookshelf it's a different—

RENATA ADLER

It's just the light. The light. Why should there be a source of light in what you're reading? It doesn't seem natural to me. And I just think technology has advanced so much it's doing us physical harm.

12

Mark Strand & Charles Wright

MARK STRAND

How are you tonight?

CHARLES WRIGHT

I'm fine. I love what you read tonight.

MARK STRAND

I love what you read, too, but I'd already read it before.

CHARLES WRIGHT

This is the way people stay friends.

MARK STRAND

We can talk about the old days in Iowa City or we can talk about why Charles continues to write and why I don't. Charles has many more ideas than I have.

CHARLES WRIGHT

That's bullshit and you know it. I haven't written in two years until this summer, and then I went crazy and wrote a lot of bad stuff. But it doesn't matter.

MARK STRAND

Oh, no, but it's good.

CHARLES WRIGHT

Well, thank you, Mark. I want to know is anyone here older than us, and I don't think so. So we can say whatever the hell we want, can't we?

MARK STRAND

And we can say it and get away with it. What do you want to say, Charles?

CHARLES WRIGHT

I want to say that I do love those prose pieces.

MARK STRAND

Well, some of you had heard what I read before. I haven't written anything new. I tried, last night, but it didn't turn out well. I should say that if I thought what I am about to read was poetry, I never would have written it. I thought I was writing prose. But then people keep talking about "those prose poems." They used the word "poem" so often that now I've begun to refer to them as poems, although I'm going to try not to tonight. I'm going to refer to them as prose pieces. I had fun writing them. I should talk about myself, or what was myself, when I was writing the prose pieces. But of course I'm entirely different now. So many changes. My hair is getting red again. I'm getting shorter. But

I had so much fun writing the prose pieces, the kind of fun I never really had writing poetry. Well, I did when I first started writing poetry, and the poems came easily. But then, as the years went on, they didn't come so easily, and when they don't come easily, you begin to wonder, "Am I really a poet?" Because poets should be able to write poems. I would have these periods of two to three years when I didn't write. This caused a degree of anxiety in me, so that whenever I did sit down to write a poem there was an enormous amount of pressure on me to succeed. I would feel that I was on to something some of the time, but after I'd been writing for a while, I'd begin to see the limitations of what I was writing and lose heart. Sometimes I was able to sustain the illusion that this was a valuable poem I was writing.

So, the writing of the prose pieces, because I thought they were prose—and I still believe they are prose—liberated me from that kind of pressure. It also allowed me to be funnier—because I think I am terribly funny—than I would allow myself to be in a poem. I've always thought poetry was a serious business. And I shouldn't say business, because you don't make any money from poetry. If it's a business, it's a bad business.

The difference is the prose pieces don't have the weight, the words don't have the specific gravity. There's a lightness about that book. I wish it were more leaden and heavier! In other words, I don't want you to feel disappointed, because even though I say that about the book, it is a totally brilliant effort. No one else could have done it. Nobody else probably would want to do it. Anyway, that's the story of my writing life. Now, Charles, tell us the story of your writing life.

CHARLES WRIGHT

Fair's fair. I can't write prose, so I don't have the escape Mark has. I can't paint. I used to play golf.

MARK STRAND

You were good.

CHARLES WRIGHT

I was good, but I'm not anymore. So poems are the only thing I have. And since they don't tell stories, they're mostly meditations about what I want to think is going on in my head and in my life at any given time. And so I write that down. There was always a sense of urgency about writing poems, about trying to get said what you felt should be said about things and yourself and your relation to them, and your relation to what is there and is not there. The urgency always held sway. Two years ago, the urgency took a hike. And that's okay, but urgency is really important in poetry, to feel that you have to write it. If you don't feel that, then don't write poetry. There seems to be no reason to write poetry if you don't have to, or want to. There are plenty of other people doing it. You can't walk down the street without getting hit with fifteen poets, even on the cross streets.

Just to drop a name, I once read that Seamus Heaney said that poems should not come out of habit, but out of necessity. But after a certain period of time, after you've said the one or the four or five things that you probably have to say in your life, and you've said them five or six different ways, over forty years—you ought to, as my wife says, lay your pen aside. You ought to shut up.

Then, this summer, I picked it back up again after two years, and wrote the apocrypha to my last book, which has just been finished. I'm sort of like Mark, I don't know if I'll ever write a poem again. But then I can't write essays, I can't write short stories, I can't even write letters anymore. It bores me to death to write letters, though I used to write them all the time. That leaves me high and dry, sitting on top of my fifty published books, so water can stay down there.

When we started out, it was fun, Mark. We used to take our poems into the bar every night, and show them to everybody, as if everybody cared about them, but no one would care about what they said. Then after a while, after about twenty years, I never showed them to anybody, ever again. Even my publisher, he wouldn't look at them. He'd just put them into covers. I probably could write something else, but I won't, because I'm lazy.

MARK STRAND

Well, there's the other thing. We are lazy. I am lazy. And now I know that you may be lazy in the future.

Questions from the Audience

I'd like to ask you both, if you had decided you were not becoming a poet, what else would you have done in life?

CHARLES WRIGHT

Well, everybody always says that at an early age they had this great ambition to do this or that. But I had no ambition in my life whatsoever, except for the next beer and the next girl. That's all I cared about. And the next golf game. That was really all I had. It wasn't until I was twenty-three years old, and in the Army, when I was stationed in Italy, that I read this poem. I'd always sort of wanted to write, but that's not wanting to do anything. But then I read this poem, and it really got to me. I thought maybe I could do something like that. It wasn't narrative, and it was beautiful. Only years later I found out that it was in iambic pentameter, which is why it sounded so good. I tried imitating that, and that's how I got going.

I guess I wanted to be a journalist, originally. To get out of the Army early, I applied to the Columbia Graduate School of Journalism, uptown, and lo and behold, I got in. But I really got caught by the throat with poetry. And it was fortunate that it was something I could write, since I didn't have to tell a story. Southerners are supposed to be able to tell a story, but I can't, my father couldn't, my brother couldn't, my mother couldn't . . . Actually, nobody in my family could tell a story, and so I'd never heard them.

There I was, floating around in the Army, having the time of my life in Italy, a country that blew me away, because I came from the hills of east Tennessee and had never seen anything except a postcard before. It was great. I wrote to the famous Writers' Workshop at the University of Iowa, and had turned in my manuscript in August for September acceptance. I got accepted and went there.

The first word out of the first person's mouth was from Dr. Strand, here. He talked about the first poem on the first worksheet, and said the iambic pentameter was not working. Strand was pissing on the post, establishing himself, which he did, immediately. I thought I was dead meat, because I did not know what iambic pentameter was. Later I found out the reason I got in was because nobody had read my manuscript. They'd just sent my manuscript over to the graduate school. So there I was, floating around again. I attached myself to Strand. I knew I had a lot to learn, and I kept my mouth shut for two years and learned something, not enough.

They taught us in Iowa never to use an abstract word like "unseeable." But that was fifty-one years ago. I don't think it makes any difference now. You go to graduate school, learn a lot of stuff, and spend the rest of your life getting rid of it. It's fun, playing cards above the bar.

MARK STRAND

Well, I wanted to be a painter and went to art school. Everybody there seemed to have much more talent than I had. Then I read poetry and I established myself as a loudmouth. The teacher would talk about our paintings, and I would say, "Well, Hazlitt talks about gusto in these terms." And the poor professor didn't know what to make of that. I was a pretentious little twit, a show-off, all because I knew deep down I just didn't have that much talent. I had to do something to make myself present. I really loved what some of my fellow students were doing, and after my first year, I just settled for peaceful anonymity, a kind of narcosis of the spirit. I slept through the last couple of years of art school. I then went to Italy on a Fulbright in Literature, and I started writing. I woke up when I was forty and realized I couldn't be a waiter in a restaurant anymore, as my feet would hurt. I had to keep writing, because I could sit down and do it. Now I'm . . . forty-four. That's my story.

This is a question initially for Mr. Strand, but I think it applies to Mr. Wright, too. I've always felt there is a really strong narrative component in your poems. I always thought your poems come from a certain idea, and that you start developing it into the depth that you were talking about. I would like to ask if in your recent works you show a bit of that procedure.

MARK STRAND

This is another way of putting that it, that they're not finished poems.

But they're finished prose.

MARK STRAND

You're absolutely right. It's easier to write these because I don't have to carry them to the next stage. Although a few of them were written from rough drafts I had of poems that I knew I couldn't finish. I used some of those rough drafts of poems that had been around for years, in some cases, and I just wrote them as prose, in a paragraph. I could live with that, because my expectations for prose aren't what they are for poetry. Simple as that.

CHARLES WRIGHT

There is a little darkness running under all of these prose pieces, like a little stream running, and you shouldn't discount that. Yes, they're funny; yes, they're sometimes amazingly funny and gross at the same time. But there is a seriousness under all of these things. From that point of view, don't discount this, *Almost Invisible*. My next book is going to be *Long Gone*.

MARK STRAND

Oh, I thought it might be *Invisible*, like mine.

CHARLES WRIGHT

No, I'm not coming back.

MARK STRAND

We're both valedictory poets. We've been waving goodbye for a while, Charles.

When you look at a poem and thought it had value, what made you feel that way?

MARK STRAND

Do you mean my poems or anybody's poems? In the case of mine, it's when they wanted a certain magic, a certain element that you could feel was there but you couldn't really put your finger on it. You look for a poem that had a life that was present, but at the same time was unreachable. That it existed in this world but had a foot in the other world, whatever that other world is. That there was something in the poem that drew you in to another level of knowledge, but you didn't quite know what that was.

CHARLES WRIGHT

Or that you didn't know that you knew.

MARK STRAND

Or that you didn't know that you knew. I think that's one of the things about writing. You write, and you wonder, "Did I write that?" Or, "Wow, I didn't know I could say that." When you write you sometimes follow formal imperatives, you feel the rightness of what you're doing even though you don't understand it. You really can't paraphrase. You just feel the weight of it. You feel its presence.

CHARLES WRIGHT

I feel the same way. That magic, what you say is magic, is also magic to me. But it's also an entrance point to something beyond what I'm able to say. What I'm always trying to do is to get to it in the most interesting way that I can. I want to get to that point, that still point that's beyond what I know, and where I'll never see, but I like to know I'm looking for it.

Mr. Strand, when I read your prose pieces, I wondered whether they would lean towards poetry or towards prose. Today, when you read,

I thought you were reading poetry, because there was one very strong element of rhythm.

MARK STRAND

If you've been writing poetry for fifty years, it's hard to shake it. My prose is rhythmical because it's the way I think. I can't help it.

CHARLES WRIGHT

The difference between *Mr. and Mrs. Baby* and *Almost Invisible*, the prose is quite striking. These pieces are short, which gives to them the idea that the compression is a poetic compression. I've known Mark a long time, and these are prose pieces, no matter how he reads them. Except that one about the Spanish poet, which is a poem.

MARK STRAND

There is a poem in that. I wanted to write something that sounded like a translation of Lorca. I can't read that poem in Spain, because in Spanish it just seems like a lousy poem. The horrors of translation.

How many of you were in Iowa in those days? Was Paul Engle doing the workshops? What was the atmosphere? Was it very competitive? Was it when he was doing the workshops?

MARK STRAND

Yes, Paul was the king.

CHARLES WRIGHT

Well, he ran it out of his back pocket. He raised all the money that he used to get the talented people there. Those of us just out of the Army after three years had a lot of money, so we paid our own way, but Paul would go over to Cedar Rapids, and go to the Quaker Oats Company and get money for this. He didn't really run the workshops. Donald Justice did. Paul would come in from time to time, but he was too busy raising money, keeping the thing afloat. He did establish the international workshop, which was a big thing. It was a big deal. We both got there from Italy at the same time, fall of . . . 1961? I was so smitten with Italy and I knew Mark had just been there. So I just introduced myself. I think there were thirty poets and thirty fiction writers. Now there are sixty of each.

MARK STRAND

Yes. We stayed in a barracks. It was simple in those days. We all lived for poetry. We would drink in the same bars, play pinball, play cards, and we all talked about poetry all the time.

CHARLES WRIGHT

Yes, that's all we talked about, and all you lived for. I'm sure they still do it.

MARK STRAND

Those were the good old days.

About the Contributors

Renata Adler's works of journalism include *A Year in the Dark*, *Toward a Radical Middle*, and *Canaries in the Mineshaft*, and she is the author of the novels *Speedboat*, winner of the Ernest Hemingway Award for Best First Novel, and *Pitch Dark*, both of which were reissued by NYRB Classics in 2013. She was a staff writer at the *New Yorker* from 1963 to 2001.

Edward Albee, the American playwright, was born in 1928. His plays include *A Delicate Balance*, *Seascape*, and *Three Tall Women*—all three of which won a Pulitzer Prize—as well as *Who's Afraid of Virginia Woolf?*, which won a Tony Award for Best Play.

Hilton Als is the theater critic for the *New Yorker*, where he has been a staff writer since 1994. He is the author of *The Women* and *White Girls*, and has taught at Yale University, Wesleyan, and Smith College.

Paul Auster is the best-selling author of *The New York Trilogy* and many other critically acclaimed novels. He has been awarded the

Princess of Asturias Prize for Literature, the Prix Médicis Étranger, the Film Independent Spirit Award, and the Premio Napoli. His work has been translated into more than forty languages.

Blake Bailey is the author of biographies of John Cheever, Richard Yates, and Charles Jackson, as well as *The Splendid Things We Planned*, a memoir about his family. He is at work on the authorized biography of Philip Roth. He is the recipient of a Guggenheim Fellowship and an Award in Literature from the American Academy of Arts and Letters; the winner of a National Book Critics Circle Award and the Francis Parkman Prize; and a finalist for the Pulitzer Prize.

Alison Bechdel is the author of the cult hit comic strip *Dykes to Watch Out For*, as well as two critically acclaimed graphic memoirs, *Fun Home* and *Are You My Mother?*

Tina Chang is the Poet Laureate of Brooklyn and the author of *Half-Lit Houses* and *Of Gods & Strangers*. She is the co-editor of the anthology *Language for a New Century: Contemporary Poetry from the Middle East, Asia, and Beyond* with Nathalie Handal and Ravi Shankar. Her poems have appeared in *American Poet*, *McSweeney's*, *Ploughshares*, and the *New York Times*.

Junot Díaz was born in the Dominican Republic and raised in New Jersey. He is the author of *Drown*; *The Brief Wondrous Life of Oscar Wao*, which won the Pulitzer Prize and the National Book Critics Circle Award; and *This Is How You Lose Her*, a *New York Times* bestseller and National Book Award finalist.

Deborah Eisenberg's story collections include *Transactions in a Foreign Currency*, *Under the 82nd Airborne*, *All Around Atlantis*, and

Twilight of the Superheroes. She is the recipient of a PEN/Faulkner Award for Fiction, a Whiting Writers' Award, a Guggenheim Fellowship, and a MacArthur Fellowship.

Rivka Galchen is the author of the novel *Atmospheric Disturbances* and the story collection *American Innovations.* She is the recipient of a William Saroyan International Prize for Fiction Writing and a Rona Jaffe Foundation Writers' Award, among other distinctions. She writes regularly for the *New Yorker,* whose editors selected her for their list of "20 Under 40" American fiction writers in 2010.

A. M. Homes is the author of six novels, most recently *May We Be Forgiven*, two collections of stories, and the memoir *The Mistress's Daughter.* Her fiction and essays have been published in the *New Yorker,* the *New York Times, Vanity Fair, Harper's, Granta*, and *One Story.*

Hari Kunzru is the author of the novels *Gods Without Men*, *My Revolutions*, *The Impressionist,* and *Transmission.* He is the recipient of the Somerset Maugham Award, a Galaxy British Book Award, and the Pushcart Prize, and in 2003 *Granta* named him one of its twenty best young British novelists.

Rachel Kushner, a recipient of a 2013 Guggenheim Fellowship, is the author of *Telex from Cuba* and *The Flamethrowers*, both of which were finalists for the National Book Award in Fiction. Her writing has appeared in the *New Yorker,* the *New York Times*, *Harper's*, and the *Paris Review.*

Wendy Lesser is a critic, novelist, and founding editor of the *Threepenny Review.* Lesser is the author of ten books, including *Why I Read* and the novel *The Pagoda in the Garden.*

D. T. Max, a staff writer at the *New Yorker*, is the author of *The Family That Couldn't Sleep: A Medical Mystery* and *Every Love Story Is a Ghost Story: A Life of David Foster Wallace*.

Leigh Newman is the author of *Still Points North*, which was a finalist for the National Book Critics Circle John Leonard Prize. She is the editor-at-large for Black Balloon Press and an editor at Oprah.com. She lives in Brooklyn.

Téa Obreht was born in 1985 in the former Yugoslavia and has lived in the United States since the age of twelve. She is the author of the novel *The Tiger's Wife*, and her work has appeared in *Zoetrope: All-Story*, *Harper's*, the *New York Times*, and the *New Yorker*, whose editors selected her for their list of "20 Under 40" American fiction writers in 2010.

Robert Pinsky, a former United States Poet Laureate, is the author of eight collections of poetry, including, most recently, his *Selected Poems*. His translation of *The Inferno of Dante* won the *Los Angeles Times* Book Prize in Poetry.

Katie Roiphe is the author of five books, including, most recently, *In Praise of Messy Lives: Essays*. She is Director of the Cultural Reporting and Criticism Program at NYU's Arthur L. Carter Journalism Institute.

George Saunders, a 2006 MacArthur Fellow, is the author of several collections of short stories, including *Tenth of December*, which was a finalist for the National Book Award and winner of the Story Prize.

David Shields's books include *Reality Hunger*, *The Thing About Life Is That One Day You'll Be Dead*, *Black Planet*, and *I Think*

I also want to thank my son, Lucian, who is the guiding light in my life. And a giant thanks to my father who championed me in the darkest and brightest of times.

–Jessica Strand

You're Totally Wrong. The recipient of a Guggenheim Fellowship and two NEA Fellowships, Shields has published essays and stories in the *New York Times Magazine*, *Harper's*, *Esquire*, *Yale Review*, *Village Voice*, *Salon*, *Slate*, *McSweeney's*, and *Believer.* His work has been translated into twenty languages.

Charles Simic was born in Belgrade and emigrated to the United States in 1954. A former United States Poet Laureate, he is the author of more than thirty collections of poetry and the recipient of many awards, including the Pulitzer Prize, the Griffin Poetry Prize, and a MacArthur Fellowship.

Tracy K. Smith is the author of three books of poetry: *Life on Mars*, which received the 2012 Pulitzer Prize; *Duende*, recipient of the 2006 James Laughlin Award; and *The Body's Question*, which won the 2002 Cave Canem Poetry Prize. Smith is also the recipient of a 2004 Rona Jaffe Award and a 2005 Whiting Award.

Mark Strand was a Pulitzer Prize–winning poet, essayist, and translator. A former United States Poet Laureate and MacArthur Fellow, he was the author of many books of poems, a book of stories, and three volumes of translations, and he was the editor of several anthologies. The winner of a Bollingen Prize, Strand was a professor of English and Comparative Literature at Columbia University from 2005 until his death in 2014.

Charles Wright, winner of the Pulitzer Prize, the National Book Critics Circle Award, the National Book Award, the Bollingen Prize, and the Griffin Poetry Prize, is the author of more than twenty collections of poetry. In 2014, he was named United States Poet Laureate.

Acknowledgments

It has been a long process, and without the kind nudging and support of my agent at the Wylie Agency, Jacqueline Ko, and my editor at Norton, Matt Weiland, keeping me and Andrea on course, there would be no book. Many thanks to the Strand Book Store, including Fred and Nancy Bass as well as all the peopl who helped run the audio and video, moved chairs, ran for wat and coffee, and who made things easier for me and the writ A special thanks to Kate Garber, my colleague and comrade arms at the Strand, who helped make the program a unique and most of all to all the wonderful writers and moderator participated.

Thank you to the incredible people at Norton: Sa Laughlin, Remy Cawley, Elisabeth Kerr (who introduc Matt), Nancy Palmquist, Dave Cole, Louise Mattarel Steve Attardo. Thank you to Lotta Nieminen, who ill cover. And thanks again to Matt for being so enthusias ful from the beginning.

About the Editors

Jessica Strand, former events coordinator at the Strand Book Store, is the associate director of public programs at the New York Public Library. She lives in New York.

Andrea Aguilar is a freelance journalist based in New York. She has been a contributing writer to *El País* since 2003.